TEN CATS & ONE
CRAZY
CAT
LADY

AMELIA HENDREY

First published 2024 by Wrate's Publishing

ISBN 978-1-0686952-0-9

Edited and typeset by Wrate's Editing Services
www.wrateseditingservices.co.uk

A CIP catalogue record for this book is available from the British Library.

I dedicate this book to Jude,
for always being there for my cats.
This is my thank you to you.

CONTENTS

THE BEGINNING

Welcome to the world of feline fanatics! My name is Amelia, and I am thrilled that you have picked up my book. Over the past twenty-one years, I have been lucky enough to share my life with a cohort of cats, each one with its own personality and quirks. But it's not just my own pets that have captured my heart; I have lost count of the number of times that random cats have crossed my path and I've just had to stop and say hello. From fluffy Persians to scrappy strays, each one has found a special place in my heart. I've always been fascinated by their independence, their grace and their mysterious ways. And let's not forget their purring. Is there anything more soothing than the sound of a contented cat?

So, buckle up and get ready to embark on a journey through the world of cats. Whether you're a long-time cat lover or a curious newbie, I promise there will be something to pique your interest and leave you feline fantastic.

Before we start, let me tell you a little about me. For my day job, I am a professional cat sitter, so right now I feel like the cat who got the cream. I get paid to give cuddles, scratches and snuggles to the best animals on the planet, and what could be better than that? But that isn't the start of the story, not even close. So much more happened before I became a cat sitter. So, get comfy, put your paws up and let me take you back to where it all began...

I have always carried a love for cats. Even as a child, I would wrap my little chubby arms around their necks desperate for them to love me. There's a photo of me as a toddler snuggled up with a black cat named Georgie. Apparently, I was inseparable from that kitty. I used to lay with him and follow him everywhere. I have no recollection of this, but it does sound like something I would do. I don't have any more information about Georgie, which is a shame. Maybe he was the start of it all. Who knows, maybe bonding with him was the moment that sealed my fate as a crazy cat lady in the making.

As I got older, my parents had four cats: Mac, Arthur, Stripey and Gizmo. I remember them fondly, as they were the highlight of my childhood, and I felt they understood me better than anyone else in the world. I loved waking up to find them sleeping at the foot of my bed, and they would always provide me with a good headbutt to the face to start my day. Later, they would sit with me while I watched my favourite cartoons. I'd brush their fur and give them what I thought were cool, new hairstyles. We shared a language that only we understood. They were the only friends a girl could ever need.

Cats mostly take a shine to me, too. I'll be walking along the street when one will randomly appear from nowhere, tail bolt upright in the air, and start headbutting my legs, meowing and wanting to be stroked. How do they know I'm a cat person? Maybe they can sense it, or perhaps it's just a coincidence. Who knows. Either way, I love it when it happens.

Speaking of love, I have a soft spot for cat-themed books, especially if they have a furry, little protagonist as the main character. One book that still sticks with me is *Stray* by A. N. Wilson, which was first published in 1987. It follows the story of a small kitten who becomes a stray after being thrown out of a

moving car. The story is told from the cat's perspective, how he sees the world, the adventures he has, and the friendships he makes along the way. It was one of the first books that tugged at my heart strings, and it has stayed with me through to adulthood.

My life growing up in the 80s and 90s was filled with fictional cats of all shapes and sizes, from the classic poem *The Owl and the Pussy-Cat* to the quirky Cheshire Cat in *Alice in Wonderland*. And let's not forget about the iconic TV cats like Garfield, Tom from *Tom and Jerry* and *Postman Pat's* trusty sidekick, Jess. It's no wonder I'm not a dog person!

The 90s was also a golden era for movie cats. My favourites included Thackery Binx in *Hocus Pocus* and Sassy in *Homeward Bound*. Watching them on screen taught me valuable life lessons, such as how to chase my dreams, the importance of a good nap, and that sometimes it's OK to be a scaredy cat.

If there is one thing my daughter has inherited from me, it's our mutual love of all things feline. She was born in 2013, on the purrfect day for a kitty lover – International Cat Day (8th August). As soon as I found out, I knew this was destiny at work, and it filled me with hope that one day she might be as cat crazy as her dear old mum.

While she may not quite be ready to throw cat-themed birthday parties just yet, she's already developed a taste for the finer things in feline literature. She has her own set of cat books that she adores, including the *Mog* series by Judith Kerr and a range of other beautifully illustrated tales chronicling cats and their adventures.

Perhaps the most fascinating book she owns is a cat encyclopaedia. It's a treasure trove of information about different cat breeds and their unique characteristics and behaviours. There is so much to read that she is always learning something new. I can

see the spark of fascination in her eyes when she flips through the pages, and it fills me with joy to think she is sharing my passion.

I am an avid reader of *Your Cat* magazine, which has been running since 1994 and covers everything from feline health and nutrition to rescue stories, cat shows and cat-friendly places to visit. What's more, I love flipping to the 'Pawtraits' section, where readers share adorable snaps of their kitties. On a couple of occasions, I have been fortunate enough to have my own cats featured in this section. I treasure my collection of *Your Cat*, not only for its engaging content, but also as a future resource for my daughter to enjoy and learn from.

My husband also shares my passion for cats and feline welfare and, in June 2006, we embarked on a nine-mile walk to raise money for the esteemed Cats Protection organisation. History has a way of repeating itself and, in May 2023, my daughter and I carried on this noble tradition by participating in a spirited, three-mile run for the same UK charity.

So, picture this: a young girl with a passion for cats grows up to be a full-blown crazy cat lady with not one, not two, but *ten* cats living with her at the same time! That's right, ten. It's not like I planned to have that many, but life is full of surprises, right?

Now, you may be thinking that having ten cats is just insane! But let me tell you, it's been pure bliss. The memories I created with them are priceless, so much so that I was inspired to write this book. But don't worry, it's not just a boring list of cat names and descriptions. My book is filled with the heart-warming stories they helped to create. It also shows off their individual characters and personalities. And I've added plenty of cat photos to make you feel like you're right there with us. I've also recounted the tales (or should that be tails?) of my travels to meet other cat crazy people around the world. These include a visit to Amsterdam, where I discovered a harmonious community of felines living on a canal boat, despite the supposed aversion that cats have to water, and Rome, where I called at a cat sanctuary amidst the breathtaking, ancient ruins. Closer to home, I stopped for a cuppa at a dedicated London cat café, where 'me time' has been replaced with 'cat play and bonding time'.

After reading this introduction, you are no doubt wondering how many cats you need in your life to be a member of the crazy cat lady club. Maybe reading my book will help you decide!

1
ISIS

When I first met Isis, she was already nine years old. She was my husband Dave's cat and he had raised her from a kitten. He named her Isis after the Egyptian goddess because he happened to be visiting the Temple of Isis on the day she was born.

Isis came from humble beginnings; her parents were farm cats who worked hard to keep down the rodent population. When they had a litter of kittens, they were sold for a cheap price, and that's how my Dave came to have her.

As a kitten, Isis showed her adventurous side by climbing straight to the top of the Christmas tree and basking in the glory of the decorations. She would occasionally peek out to admire her handiwork and show off her tree-climbing prowess.

Isis had a way of captivating everyone she met. Her striking black fur, sleek and shiny, seemed to absorb all the light around her, making her stand out even more. But it was her deep green eyes that really drew people in – they were so incredibly expressive and seemed to carry a deep wisdom beyond what it's believed cats possess.

And then there was her purr – more than a happy sound, it was a force to be reckoned with! When she got going, her whole body would vibrate with the intensity of it, and you couldn't help but feel the love radiating from her. She would sit on your chest, her face millimetres from yours, her head rocking to the sound of her own purr.

Isis had a real head for heights. Dave had two trees in his garden, and he nailed a piece of wood between them to form a bridge for her to play on. She would climb up one tree, run across the plank of wood, and then go down the other side, repeating this process over and over. When she wasn't busy climbing, she used to sit on the plank watching the birds, or else she would lay there enjoying the sun on her face and the breeze in her fur.

Six months after getting Isis, Dave visited a cat rehoming centre and fell in love with a male, British shorthair kitten whom he named Zeus. Zeus was pure grey, with a stocky build. Isis wasn't sure about him at first, but Zeus was determined to win her over, and boy did he achieve his aim.

As it turned out, Zeus was quite the gentleman. Whenever it was feeding time, he would patiently wait for Isis to finish her meal before digging in himself. How he managed to resist the temptation of that delicious cat food smell for so long we will never know, but one thing for sure is that Zeus was a true class act.

His impeccable manners paid off and Isis accepted him as her friend, and they went on to become great buddies. He loved nothing more than lounging around in the great outdoors. He would snooze the day away under bushes or on top of bungalow roofs, not a care in the world.

Sadly, Zeus's life was cut short due to an incurable health condition. At just six years old, he developed a blood clot in his lower back that stopped his hind legs from working. While I never got to meet Zeus in person, he lives on in the memories and photos shared by those who knew and loved him the best.

Following the loss of Zeus, Isis became a lone wolf and didn't show any interest in befriending other felines. It was evident that she missed her furry companion, as he was the only cat she ever let her guard down for.

Isis was a cat with a personality like no other. Her love for Dave was obvious as she followed him around the house, always finding a way to curl up on his lap or next to him on the sofa. Her delicate appearance and tiptoe walk made her seem like a ballerina gliding across the room, and her claws on her back feet were always out, creating a distinct sound on the wooden floor that meant you could always hear her coming.

But it was her love for cheese that was truly remarkable. As soon as the fridge door opened, she would be there in a flash, hoping to get her paws on some Red Leicester. She would meow and stand on her hind legs, reaching up with her front paws, eager to get a bite. And once she had it, she would purr contentedly as she savoured every morsel.

But cheese wasn't her only chewable love; she was also partial to raw chicken wings. She liked to really gnaw on the bone, getting every last bit of the meat off it, which the vet assured us would help keep her teeth clean.

Isis was one of those cats who made it her mission to find the sunniest spot, no matter what time of day it was; if the sun was out, she was out. She would spend hours lounging on her back with her legs up in the air, soaking up all those rays. And if the sun happened to disappear behind a cloud? No worries, she would just move to the next sunny spot she could find. And on the rare occasion she couldn't be bothered to venture outside, she had a backup plan – the windowsill. She would stretch out as far as she could, determined to catch every ray of sunshine that came through the glass.

It's a good thing my husband is a builder and not an inventor, because he missed the opportunity to take the next big cat toy to

market. He used to cut off bits of plastic wire, twist them into a spring and throw it across the floor for Isis to play with. She would have hours of fun chasing it, scooting around and batting it with her delicate paws. Little did we know that someone else had the same idea and turned it into a sellable cat toy.

Isis was a picture of perfect health and her annual check-ups at the vets were a breeze. However, she did eventually develop one minor issue that bothered us. One of her front teeth was wobbly and seemed to be hanging from her mouth like a loose thread. We waited a week hoping it would fall out when she ate, but to no avail. So, we took her to the vet. As soon as the vet opened her mouth, and to our great surprise, the tooth simply fell out. So, that proved a simple fix. Apart from that, Isis didn't have any other health problems, for which we were truly grateful.

As you already know, Isis loved climbing, and she soon became bored with scaling trees; so she took it to the next level by tackling ladders. Whenever we had one propped up against the house, she would be the first one up there surveying her kingdom like the feline queen she clearly was. One day, we were having some work done on the house and had some scaffolding put up. It hadn't been there for more than an hour when we spotted Isis walking around on it, inspecting everything with the utmost curiosity. It was like she was the foreman of the project, making sure everything was up to scratch. And just like that, she made her way back down effortlessly – just another day in the life of a daredevil cat. We often wondered why she was so keen on being up high. Was she planning her next adventure or simply enjoying the view?

One evening, as Isis lay in her bed on the kitchen floor, I immediately spotted that something wasn't right. She looked up at me with her bright eyes, but she didn't want to move. My heart sank as I watched her lying there, unable to understand what was happening. I gave her a piece of cheese, hoping it would perk her up, but she didn't take it. It was most unlike her to show no interest in her favourite treat.

Dave and I decided to take her to the vet, worried that something serious might be happening. But as I held her on my lap in the car on the way there, she suddenly let out a scream and passed away in my arms. She was old by this point and had never suffered any major health problems. I think it might have been a stroke or a heart attack. I feel like she had an amazing life and that this was just her time. But that didn't at all lessen the pain of losing her. We took her home and buried her in the garden next to her favourite sunny spot, along with a flower and a piece of cheese. She was a couple of months off making it to her 20th birthday.

She is missed every day.

ISIS

**We had a glass plaque made with her photo and an inscription.
It reads:**

Life will never be the same without you.
We will never be the same without you.
You will always be priceless.
R.I.P ISIS X
1992–2012

2

SHUSH

Have you ever made a spontaneous decision that ended up being one of the best of your life? Well, Shush was one of mine.

Dave and I had been discussing getting a kitten for weeks, and when we finally made the decision to go for it, I couldn't contain my excitement. The thought of another furry little friend to share our home with filled me with joy. We came across an ad for some kittens in London; it was a bit of a journey to the capital, but we didn't mind, as we were so eager to find the perfect puss to join our family.

When we arrived, there was only a single female kitten left; a tiny, white ball of fluff with three, distinctive black cow-print spots and big green eyes. She had a little black moustache under her nose and a full black tail. I gently stroked her soft fur and watched as she batted my fingers with her tiny paws. It was clear she was already comfortable with us and that we were meant to be her forever home.

We decided on the name Shush, as it's the noise I made to her as she meowed in the car all the way back from London. Once Shush was in the door, she wasted no time settling in. She explored her new surroundings with a curious and adventurous spirit, quickly making herself at home.

One of the first things she did was to approach Isis. Although Isis was initially wary of the new arrival, Shush didn't seem to mind, and she sniffed around, trying to get to know the queen of the house. And even though Isis hissed and swatted at her, Shush persisted in trying to make friends. We knew it would take some time for Isis to adjust to having a new cat on her territory, as she was used to being the only feline in the house, and it would take patience and understanding to help her get used to a new companion. But we were confident that, with time, they would learn to coexist peacefully and perhaps even become mates.

To give Shush a quiet place to relax, we set up a cosy cardboard box for her, complete with a soft blanket to snuggle up in. But it didn't take Shush long to show us her independent streak. On the second night, she jumped out of her box and sauntered up the stairs to our bedroom, where she meowed on the floor next to our bed. Considering Shush was a tiny kitten in a big new house, we were both surprised and delighted by her bravery. As soon as we scooped her up and placed her on the bed, she knew she was home. She cuddled up between us, purring contentedly as she drifted off to sleep.

From that moment on, Shush never looked back. She had claimed her spot in our bed and in our hearts, becoming a beloved member of our family. Even Isis slowly grew to accept her, though she still maintained her distance.

A few weeks later, we scheduled Shush's first trip to the vet for her injections. Little did we know what was in store for us.

Once checked over, the vet informed us that Shush wasn't the little girl kitten we thought we had taken in – but a little boy. My husband and I were shocked at this revelation, wondering how we had missed such an important detail, yet we couldn't help but laugh at the situation. Shush, on the other hand, seemed oblivious to the gender swap and continued to be his adorable self. Despite the mix up, we felt the name Shush was still perfect for him, so decided to stick with it.

As a playful kitten, Shush had a knack for climbing up my trousers and onto my shoulder, where he would perch like a parrot. I'd stroll around the house with my furry little friend on my shoulder, feeling his tiny paws tapping against my skin as he happily surveyed his surroundings. He relished this special bonding time with me and would stay put for as long as I let him. It was heart-warming to have this little companion by my side, even if it meant constantly checking for any rogue claws digging into my clothes.

One hilarious evening, while in our bedroom, Shush was playing around on the floor when he caught sight of himself in the mirrored wardrobe. His tail puffed up like a giant feather boa and he stared at his reflection, convinced it was another cat invading his turf. He launched himself sideways and started darting back and forth, trying to make himself look as big and as intimidating as possible, to scare off his competitor. I couldn't help but laugh as I watched him do his fluffy dance. It was as if he was auditioning for *Dancing with the Feline Stars*.

Shush was always finding new ways to entertain himself. One of his favourite toys was a pom-pom attached to a coiled stand, which he would bat back and forth, determined to lift it off the ground with his teeth. It was a sight to behold, watching his little body strain with effort as he attempted to carry the toy onto the sofa. But Shush was persistent, and even though he never quite succeeded, his determination was admirable.

His all-time favourite toy was Woozel, a cute and fuzzy, weasel-shaped cat toy that he'd toss in the air and catch with ease. Shush loved sleeping with Woozel, and he often snuggled up

with his paws wrapped around it. He would carry it from room to room in his mouth, and when it was misplaced, he would stand and mew until someone found it for him. It was touching to see how attached Shush was to his toy, and my husband and I would happily launch a full-scale search to reunite him with his beloved companion.

I used to love watching Isis play 'hide and seek' on the windowsill behind the net curtain. Shush, clueless as ever, would barge in and start grooming himself, totally unaware of his feline friend's clever camouflage. But as soon as he spotted a bird and pressed his nose against the curtain to get a better look, Isis would hiss like a furious dragon and send a poor, startled Shush flying off the windowsill.

One morning, Shush's third eyelid was showing. Cats have three eyelids, and the third one is white. If it's on display, it usually means they are unwell. Plus, Shush was making a funny grunting sound while purring. We rushed him to the vet who discovered a rare polyp in the back of his throat. The vet asked if they could record the procedure to remove it, for training purposes. While we agreed, we couldn't help but worry about our little guy.

Thankfully, the surgery was successful and Shush soon bounced back. After just a few weeks, he was running around and playing like nothing had ever happened. We were so relieved to see him back to his usual self and grateful for the skilled care he had received.

Our furry little friend had a unique way of showing affection – he would knead on us with both paws, as if he was playing the world's smallest piano. We called him our little purring pianist. But that's not all. He would also unleash a Niagara Falls-like dribble, drenching us with every knead of his paws and those claws of steel. Let's just say we've had better back massages from a cactus. After a few minutes of this torture, he would shake his head, and we'd be caught in a crossfire of kitty drool. It was like we needed a poncho just to cuddle with him! But we couldn't resist his purring charms – even if it meant walking around with damp clothing all day.

A few months later, I taught him to jump into my arms, which was such a novelty and very cute. He continued to do this as he grew older and heavier, which was painful but still just as funny. He'd then climb up onto my shoulders and sit there like he used to do as a kitten, playing the piano with his paws to show how much he loved being up there.

Shush had a purr that was truly one of a kind; it wasn't just a simple hum or a vibration, it was a whole symphony of sound that seemed to come straight from the depths of his soul, filling the room with warmth and happiness.

As he grew older, Shush resembled a little boxer, with a swagger in his step that made him look like the king of the neighbourhood. He was a proper tomcat, with a tough and confident attitude that allowed him to fearlessly wander about, unconcerned by the world around him. When it came to playing, he was equally impressive. His strength was palpable, and you could feel the raw power in his paws whenever he grabbed a toy. But despite his muscular build, he was always gentle with us and our other cats, never using his strength in a way that could cause harm. Shush was a force to be reckoned with, but he only used his might for good, and we loved him all the more for it.

One day, a neighbour knocked on my door and asked if Shush belonged to me. I confirmed he did and, to my surprise, she explained that for the past few months, Shush had been secretly sneaking into her house and cuddling up on her bed with her own two cats. Despite being caught red-handed, Shush had charmed his way into her heart. It was important to my neighbour that we knew where he was when he wasn't at home. She spoke highly of Shush, complimenting his friendly nature and beautiful personality. From that day on, our cat lived a double life, splitting his time between my house and my neighbour's place.

Back then, taking my six cats out for a stroll was a regular routine. Picture this: a group of six cats walking around the block, all following their human mama like a bunch of loyal soldiers. No leads, no harnesses, just a spontaneous feline parade. It always drew curious stares from passers-by, but who cares, the cats were having a blast. And you know who would join the gang when we passed by the neighbour's house? None other than the one and only Shush. I would call out to him, and he would race to join us like Usain Bolt. He was a master of climbing trees, and while the other cats would try to catch up with him, he was too quick and agile for them. When he'd had enough of the tree, he would fly down it and zoom past me like a furry missile. We'd eventually make our way back home and the cats would either head to their food bowls or return to their cosy beds.

Shush was a true father figure to the kittens in the house, and he never showed any frustration or impatience when it came to his feline proteges. As a matter of fact, he welcomed them with open paws and would often snuggle up to them to provide a warm, protective presence. His gruff exterior belied his soft heart, and he relished being a mentor to the younger generation.

When it came to playtime, Shush was the master of improvisation. He could turn a box or a carrier bag into a world of adventure and excitement. He would hide inside them and ambush the kittens with gentle taps before rolling onto his side to invite them to play with his paws. It was a joy to see how he revelled in the simple pleasures of playtime, and how he passed on that love of life to his siblings.

One scorching summer day, Shush returned home with a whole raw sausage clenched firmly in his jaws, as if he had just robbed a local butcher. As he proudly jumped over the back gate, Dave and I couldn't help but chuckle at his brazen attitude. We joked that maybe he had raided someone's barbeque and made off with the prized meat. Although we never found out the true source of his bounty, we were grateful that he had managed to escape without being caught in the act. As a true adventurer, Shush loved to explore the great outdoors, rain or shine, but he always made it back home just in time for dinner.

As an adult, Shush loved boxes, and he would try to wedge himself into even the smallest ones. Nine times out of ten, he would be successful. Once, we put a McDonald's Happy Meal box on the floor just to see what he would do. He immediately went over to it, tipped it on its side and put his head in it. After realising this was the best he was going to get from it, he sat there for an hour, finally falling asleep. I think he must have felt a real sense of achievement.

Shush was full of surprises, and we never knew where we would find him sleeping next. Sometimes, we would come down to the bathroom to find him snuggled up in the sink, as if it was the most natural thing in the world. He had a cosy cat bed and activity centre, but the sink became his new favourite spot. Perhaps he just fancied a break from his usual sleeping arrangements. And when he did sleep, he slept in the most awkward yet adorable positions, such as upside down in the activity centre with his body dangling out. It was if he was saying, "I know I look ridiculous, but I am so comfortable right now, so leave me be."

I got home from work one day and noticed something off with my Shush. His usually bright and alert eyes were sunken, and his head seemed unnaturally swollen. In an instant, I knew something

was seriously wrong. I rushed him to the vet, who said he had developed an abscess behind his nose and eyes after being in a fight. I agreed to the necessary treatment, which involved draining the abscess and providing him with pain relief. Despite looking like a champion boxer following the incision, Shush didn't let it get him down for long. He spent the next week feeling sorry for himself and demanding extra cuddles, but before we knew it, he was back to his normal laid-back self.

I have another story to demonstrate how laid-back Shush was. During a decorating project, we started tearing off the living room wallpaper as Shush napped peacefully on the floor. He continued to snooze even as the debris started landing on him. He remained in his slumber, covered in bits of wallpaper, without a care in the world. Even after we cleared the paper off him, he stayed in his spot and slept soundly. While he was snoozing, you could rest your head on him, and he would simply give a small chirp and start purring without budging an inch. It was clear that nothing could disrupt his love for a good nap.

Three years later, after settling into a new home, we received an unexpected call from a lovely lady named June. It was hard not to feel a sense of déjà vu when she said that Shush had been frequenting her garden every day, and charming her and her husband Dave with his friendly demeanour. It didn't take long for Shush to make himself at home in their house, and he would waltz in as if he owned the place. June wanted to make sure he wasn't lost and, after confirming he was mine, she welcomed him in with open arms.

Shush also made himself right at home in her pot plants, and when the plants grew too big for him to squeeze in, he would simply move onto another pot. Eventually, he graduated to June's summerhouse, where he would snooze on the bed with their own cat, Pippi. Whenever he wanted a change of scenery, he would simply wander back to ours.

June and her husband, Dave, had fallen for Shush's quirky personality, and we were grateful they accepted him as part of their family. They loved him as much as I did and took excellent care of him. We would call to check on him and June would report he was happy lounging in the sun. It was comforting to know that Shush had found another place to call home and that, just like ours, it was filled with love and affection.

One fateful morning, I found my beloved Shush crying out in pain and writhing on the sofa. I could see that he couldn't move his back legs, so I acted fast and rushed him to the vet. After a thorough examination, the vet said he suspected a blood clot in Shush's back, leaving him paralysed. In a bid to save him, the vet put him on medication and a drip and ordered me to go home, promising to update me regularly on his condition. Being away from Shush was unbearable, and my mind constantly raced over what fate had in store. The wait felt like an eternity, all I could do was hope and pray for his recovery. The next day, the vet called to say that Shush was doing better, though he was still on medication and a drip. They promised to call me the next day with a further update. My hopes were high, and it seemed his condition could be turned around.

But the news I received the next morning shattered me into a million pieces. Overnight, Shush had passed away in his sleep. I was utterly devastated and couldn't believe that he was gone forever. I had so many questions. How had this happened, and what could I have done to prevent it? I never got the chance to say goodbye to Shush or tell him how much I loved him. The grief was overwhelming, and I struggled to come to terms with the loss.

When I went to collect Shush from the vet, I wrapped him in a soft towel, held him close to my chest and cried silently. I kissed his fur and told him how much he meant to me, and how sorry I was that I couldn't save him. I knew that he had led a beautiful life and was loved by so many people.

We buried him in our garden, and I placed an ornament on his grave, depicting a cat with wings. His memory will forever remain in our hearts, and he will always be missed.

He was 14 years old.

His glass plaque reads:

If love could have saved you, you would have lived forever.
We will love you forever.
Sleep well, my fur baby.
R.I.P SHUSH X
2002–2016

3

SHAKIRA

We made the decision to bring another kitten into our household so that Shush would have a companion to grow up with. It was evident that Isis wasn't interested in playing or spending time with him, despite his attempts to bond, so we wanted to make sure that Shush had a furry friend who could match his energy levels and give him the love and attention he deserved.

We arranged to visit some cats for sale and were introduced to a number of feline residents housed in various enclosures. As we made our way through the assortment, my husband spotted a small kitten tucked away in the back who seemed to be struggling to get noticed among her more outgoing contemporaries. He asked to hold her, and as soon as my eyes landed on her, I knew she was the one. Her striking calico coat – a beautiful blend of white, orange, and black – and her enchanting green eyes made her look like a superstar, so it seemed fitting to name her after the popular singer Shakira. She was purrfect in every way.

Calico cats are more than just a pretty face – they are also a symbol of good fortune, and if you happen to come across a male calico, consider yourself extra fortunate, as they are a rare and precious gem in the feline world.

Our first night with Shakira was quite the adventure. This little ball of fur wanted to be by our side all the time and we couldn't resist her charms. She quickly hit it off with Shush, but Isis was having none of it and continued to hiss and sniff at her new family member. As bedtime approached, we set up a cosy bed and litter tray for Shakira in our room. However, she had different plans – she wanted to sleep with us! Despite her tiny size, she was determined to make it up to our bed, though she needed a little help from me. As soon as she had snuggled up, she started to purr like a mini motorboat and promptly fell asleep.

But our peaceful slumber was short-lived. The next morning, we woke to a rather unpleasant surprise. Shakira had pooed on the bed and been marching in it while we were asleep. We quickly realised her eyes were shut tight with goo, which made it impossible for her to see where she was going. After cleaning her up and washing her feet, she was able to see again, and her joy was restored. Looking back, we think Shakira was probably the runt of the litter as she was so tiny. But thankfully, a visit to the vet confirmed she was perfectly healthy. She may have been small, but she had a heart full of love that could fill a room.

Shakira and Shush were like Batman and Robin, always ready to save the day. Once, Shakira got herself in a sticky situation after climbing a tree in our garden and finding herself unable to get back down. She was meowing frantically from a branch, looking like a feline superhero in distress. That's when Shush sprang into action, climbing up after her and attempting to carry her down by the scruff of her neck. Unfortunately, it didn't quite work out, so we had to bring out the ladder and rescue the dynamic duo ourselves. Shakira was grateful and Shush got all the credit for his valiant effort.

Shakira had a mischievous side to her and regularly puffed up her fur and walked sideways, as if ready for a ninja attack. It was hilarious to watch her sneak up on Shush. Shush would run at her, and then Shakira would jump sideways, playfully trying to take him down. Even though she was smaller, she managed to pull off the ninja moves a few times, which was a sight to behold.

Shakira had a unique meow that always made us laugh. It was a cross between a meow and a squeak, and every time she did it, it sounded like she was trying to imitate a bird. We thought it was adorable, but we wanted to make sure there wasn't an underlying issue. So, when we took her to the vet for her yearly check-up, we thought it best to mention her funny meow. After a thorough examination, the vet reassured us that although Shakira had strained vocal cords, which couldn't be cured, they didn't pose a problem. From then on, we just accepted her quirky meow as part of her lovable personality.

Shakira had a hilarious quirk. If you said "bless you" after she sneezed, she would invariably sneeze again. And the funniest part? The more times you said it, the more she kept sneezing! But if you failed to say it, she would stop sneezing altogether, almost like she was waiting for your blessing. It was the weirdest thing, but we found it absolutely adorable.

Her nickname was 'Dairy Queen', and we gave her the moniker because of her insatiable appetite for yoghurt. Whenever Dave or I had one, she would appear as if out of nowhere to beg for a taste. We quickly learned that the part she was really interested in was the delicious residue left on the inside of the lid, so we would carefully peel it back and let her have it while we enjoyed our snack. It was a sweet and silly ritual that brought us all joy.

She had the cutest response whenever we sang her name. If we started singing "Shakira, Shakira" to her in the garden, she would immediately flop down and start rolling about; it was almost like a dance routine. And the best part? She would do this without fail, every single time we sang to her. It was as if she just couldn't resist the urge to boogie.

Shakira loved showing her affection. She would hop on a chair and then nudge your head with hers in a gentle headbutt. It was her way of saying, "I love you." Her little headbutt was like a tiny burst of happiness, making you feel warm and fuzzy inside.

The upstairs of my house was deemed a 'no cat's land,' and all my pets knew it. None of them were allowed upstairs on a regular basis, except Shakira – the little rebel. She had sass, and boy did she know it. Whenever I headed up to the forbidden land to do some laundry, Shakira would stealthily dart through the door and scamper up the stairs, leaving me in the dust. But that was just the beginning of her mischief.

As I climbed the stairs, my arms full of laundry, she would be lurking on the landing, ready to attack. She'd swat me through the banisters, daring me to catch her. And catch her I did, but only to return her to her rightful place downstairs.

But Shakira wasn't having any of it. She was the master of cat and mouse, and she loved the thrill of the chase. As soon as I put the laundry down and turned my back, she was back up the stairs, ready to go another round. It became a game, a hilarious back and forth that lasted for years. And no matter how many times I tried to outsmart her, Shakira always managed to get in the last swat.

Shakira was a beloved member of our family, always by our side and constantly showering us with love and affection. So, when she went missing, it was like a part of our family was missing too. We searched day and night, putting up posters and calling her name. As each day passed without any sign of her, my heart sank

deeper and deeper. I couldn't bear the thought of never seeing her again. Was she hurt? Scared? Lost?

But then after a week, in the middle of the night, I heard a faint noise in our bedroom. My heart was pounding with anticipation as I turned on the light, hoping and praying it was her. And there she was, standing in front of me looking all dirty but otherwise unharmed. I picked her up and held her close, feeling the immense relief of having her back in my arms. As she rubbed her face against mine, I felt a sense of comfort and love, which I had sorely missed. I fed her some food, which she ate quickly, and then we cuddled for hours. My girl was home, and it was a moment I will never forget; it reminded me of the powerful bond between humans and their beloved pets.

We were in for a surprise when we took Shakira to the vet to get her checked over and found out that she was pregnant. Dave immediately made it clear that we weren't keeping the kittens and made plans to rehome them once they were old enough.

Meanwhile, as Shakira's pregnancy progressed, I wanted to ensure that she had a safe and comfortable place to give birth, so I got a large box and prepared it with blankets. Despite my best efforts, Shakira didn't seem to care much for the box and avoided it entirely.

Then, nine weeks later, Shakira surprised us once again by trotting upstairs and climbing straight into the box to give birth to three gorgeous ginger and white kittens. I kept my distance, giving her the space she needed to do what came naturally, and it was a beautiful moment to witness. Shakira was a fantastic mother, and she looked after her kittens with ease, not needing any help or guidance from me.

As the kittens grew up, they formed a lovely bond with each other and Shakira kept them in check, showing them the ropes and making sure they stayed out of trouble. It was beautiful to see the love and care she naturally had for her offspring.

And now for a spoiler alert... Reader, we kept all the kittens!

After Shakira gave birth, I learned something fascinating about cats in heat. They can release multiple eggs over several days, and if they are 'courted' by more than one tom during their heat cycle, they can end up carrying kittens with multiple fathers. Even when pregnant, a female will continue to mate until their heat cycle is over. It just goes to show how amazing and complex these creatures are.

Two years after Shakira's miraculous return, she disappeared again. The morning started like any other day, but by the evening she was nowhere to be found. It was strange behaviour for her as she always liked to be in our vicinity. I couldn't shake off this bad feeling in my gut, so I cancelled my evening plans and Dave and I went out to look for her. We searched for about an hour, until we heard what sounded like a strained meow coming from a nearby bush. My heart skipped a beat as I dashed towards it to find Shakira sitting in a hole she had dug for herself. It was clear something was wrong with her hind leg – it was swinging around like it wasn't even attached. I gently lifted her up and took her home and then straight to the vets.

The vet told us it was likely that Shakira had been hit by a car, and that her leg would require surgery. He also told us that when cats feel like they are going to die and can't get home, they find a safe place away from people and animals to dig a hole in which to pass away. We were incredibly lucky to have found Shakira just in time.

She underwent surgery and returned home with metal pins in her leg, along with strict instructions to keep her in a cage and to avoid any jumping. We made sure she had a comfortable bed, food, and a litter tray in her cage, but I knew she would be bored in there. So, I got her a little portable TV, put it outside her cage and switched on a David Attenborough documentary about birds. Shakira was content to watch them fly around from the comfort of her bed.

However, a few hours later, Shakira looked at me with her big green eyes and gave me a sad, silent meow; it was clear she wanted to get out of the cage. I let her out so she could stretch her legs, but I kept a continuous eye on her, as the vet had warned us against letting her jump. She limped around the living room for a while, and then she wanted to get onto the sofa, so I carefully picked her up and set her on my lap. She loudly purred and seemed to be content with the closeness. When it was time for bed, I gently placed her back in her cage, and that became our routine until she was fully healed.

The vet also discovered that she had a heart murmur, but there was nothing we could do except monitor it. After six long months, Shakira finally healed and was back to walking without a limp. It was an incredibly challenging time, but seeing Shakira back to her normal self made it all worthwhile.

Shakira was a cat like no other, a feline who defied the norm, and she loved to do things her way. One of her favourite things was having a bath, an activity most cats would run a mile from. But not my Shakira – she would eagerly sit in the bath so I could pour warm water over her and lather her up with cat shampoo. It was the cutest thing to watch as she playfully batted at the bubbles with her paw, enjoying every moment of her spa-like experience.

Shakira had a personality so sweet and affectionate that it was hard not to think of her as a little person in a feline body. It didn't matter what we were up to – if we were doing something interesting, Shakira wanted to be right in the thick of it, eagerly participating and soaking up all the excitement.

One day, I set up a tent for my daughter to play in. Shakira wasted no time in jumping in and snuggling up alongside her. And when a bouncy castle appeared in the garden, Shakira was quick to join in the fun, bouncing around alongside the children and seemingly having the time of her life. She was so relaxed and happy-go-lucky that she even let my daughter play doctor with her, patiently letting her adorn her with stethoscopes and hats. We all loved Shakira's boundless enthusiasm and inclusive nature; it was something we had never seen in another cat.

Shakira faced a daunting challenge at the age of eleven, when she was diagnosed with gum disease and had to undergo the removal of all her teeth. As her worried owner, I couldn't help but wonder how she would cope without the essential tools for eating.

Thankfully, the vet assured me that cats' gums become hard once their teeth are removed, and that Shakira would adapt and have no trouble eating. I must admit, though, I was sceptical. How could anyone possibly be comfortable eating with no teeth? But Shakira proved me wrong in the best possible way. She took the whole ordeal in her stride, adapting to her new reality with remarkable ease. In no time at all, she was happily chowing down on all her favourite foods, completely unfazed by the lack of teeth. And over time, as her gums hardened, she even started eating biscuits, which I had assumed would be impossible.

When Shakira came into my life, I could never have imagined what an impact she would have on me. She was more than just a cat; she was my loyal friend and companion. Even now, I remember as if it was yesterday, the day I found the lump under her neck. She was 15 years old and sitting on my lap as I stroked her fur. My heart sank as I rushed her to the vet, and they confirmed it was cancer. From that day on, I did everything I could to make her remaining days comfortable and happy. Within weeks she became slower and even refused to eat at times, but I was determined to keep her spirits up. I bought all her favourite foods and even held an umbrella over her in the rain while she used the bathroom. I cherished every moment with her and hoped that she would never leave me.

However, life had other plans, and one morning, not long after she had become bedridden, I knew it was time to take her to the vet for the last time.

As I lay my head on her and said my goodbyes, my heart crumbled. She had been the best cat in the world, and I was so sorry I couldn't save her.

I buried her in the garden alongside Isis and Shush and placed a small cat ornament on her grave. Even after all these years, the memory of that day still haunts me, and I can't help but shed tears as I write this.

Shakira was one of a kind. She was beautiful inside and out, and her loving and loyal nature changed my life. Her loss left a void that can never be filled.

Her glass plaque reads:

You and me against the world, always.
R.I.P SHAKIRA X
2002–2016

4

GINGE

Ginge, a charming feline, came into this world on a beautiful spring day – April 1st, 2003 – as the son of our treasured Shakira. Ginge's striking coat was a beautiful blend of ginger and white, with elegant stripes adorning his majestic head, and intricate swirls gracing his lean, athletic body. His tail boasted eye-catching ginger swirls and, to top it all off, he had a delightful ginger smudge on his nose and mouth, adding a touch of whimsy to his already charming features.

Ginge was a cat with an unbreakable spirit, even from a young age. When his siblings were content to stay in the safety of their mother's giant box, Ginge was already looking for a way out. With determination in his heart and strength in his tiny body, he would scale the sides of the box and drop down the other side to freedom. Fearless and bold, Ginge would never hesitate to explore his new surroundings and investigate any object that caught his attention.

As he grew older, Ginge's love for the great outdoors intensified. He was the lone ranger, venturing off into the unknown to discover new sights and smells. While he wasn't the type of cat to cuddle up on your lap, he had his own unique way of showing affection. He would sometimes sit next to you, silently keeping you company until he was ready to engage in conversation. And boy could he talk. Ginge loved to meow back when spoken to, and he was always trying to have the last word with his signature three consecutive mews.

When we moved to our new house, a sinister-looking cat would often loiter in our garden, watching our cats with an angry expression. He appeared to be a stray, with matted, fluffy fur that was straggly and unkept. His dark-grey coat and old appearance made him even more intimidating. One day, I decided to try and offer him some affection, but he only glared at me with a scowl, before going on his way. But soon, strange things began to happen. The smell of cat pee permeated our home, and I knew my cats weren't responsible for it, as they were all house trained.

One night, I heard the cat flap go and witnessed the stray come in, urinate on our living room floor, and attempt to attack one of my cats. This was the moment when we discovered he had claimed our house as his territory.

After that we named him Snagglepuss, which suited him perfectly. Despite our efforts to stop him, he continued to enter our house and eat our cats' food. He would flee whenever he saw us. However, one night, we were woken by the sound of our cats screaming and fighting. When I rushed downstairs, I saw Snagglepuss fleeing through the cat flap, tufts of fur in his wake. Then I noticed that Ginge was limping. Snagglepuss had bitten his leg and the bite had fractured his ankle bone, meaning an emergency trip to the vet and an overnight stay.

After we brought Ginge home, we knew we had to take action to protect our cats. We devised a plan to block the cat flap at night using a piece of wood and some thick string. The idea was that when the string was pulled, the wood would drop down and cover the flap. We'd only do this when we knew Snagglepuss was in the house, thus giving him a fright and showing him that we were not to be messed with. We planned to release him as soon as he'd got the message. It was a foolproof plan, but Snagglepuss seemed to sense something was up, and he never returned. We waited for weeks, but there was no sign of him.

However, just as we thought we had finally won the battle, he returned with a vengeance.

As the night grew dark, a sinister sound pierced through the silence – hissing and howling coming from the living room. My heart raced and my palms went slick with sweat. I knew what this meant. Snagglepuss was back! It was time to take action. I nudged Dave, urgency in my touch, and together we prepared for battle. He grabbed the string, his muscles tense with anticipation, and let it loose with a resounding boom. The wood dropped; the beast had nowhere to go.

I dashed down the stairs, my ears ringing with the constant banging echoing through the house. As I flung open the door, my eyes darted straight for him. Snagglepuss was throwing himself at the wood, his fury fired, his determination unwavering. He was fast, but I knew he wouldn't get through.

How wrong I was. In one last massive dash, he smashed through the wood with sheer force. The wood fell from the cat flap with a thunderous crash. Snagglepuss sped into the garden, his eyes fixed on me with a fierce intensity as he kept looking back. Finally, once he reached a point which he deemed safe, he turned around and we had a staredown. Time seemed to stand still as we held each other's gaze. Then, with a flick of his tail, Snagglepuss walked away, never to enter my home again.

I saw him several times after that, walking the streets outside my house, but he never troubled us again. I knew that he had received our message loud and clear.

Ginge was always eager to explore the vast fields behind our house. Despite his adventures, he never returned home with any evidence of a catch. Our neighbours hadn't reported any sightings of him in their homes either. It was a mystery where he went or what he did during his escapades. Dave and I had a running joke that he must have been attending a secret club for cats, which we named 'The Kitty Club'.

When Ginge was just six years old, he disappeared without a trace. Our tireless effort to find him proved fruitless, and weeks turned into months. The scorching heat of the sun and the torrential downpours taunted us as we searched for our beloved friend. I feared the worst, thinking that he was gone for good. And yet, hope lingered within me. I prayed that if he was still alive, he had found a safe haven away from the brutal elements that plagued us.

Three agonising months later, we received a call. Ginge had been found, but the news was far from encouraging. A concerned passer-by had discovered him having a seizure under a car and brought him to the nearest vet. Ginge's microchip helped them locate us, but his condition was dire. He was severely malnourished, with only 10% of his body fat remaining. To survive, his body had eaten away at his own fat stores, causing him to go blind due to lack of nourishment. As if that wasn't enough, he was also suffering from neurological problems, so he had to be transferred to the Queen Mother Hospital for Animals in Hertfordshire (QMHA) for further treatment. The staff there were incredibly compassionate and understanding and gave us constant updates on his condition – we couldn't have asked for better care. Along with the person who found Ginge, we had all the staff who tirelessly treated him to thank for his life.

The vet told us they were doing everything they could to save him, but they couldn't guarantee that his sight would return. It was a waiting game to see how Ginge would recover. The vet explained to us that before he went missing, Ginge weighed a healthy 5.9kg, but now he had shrunk down to a mere 3.6kg. The gravity of his condition was all too apparent, and we were filled with a sense of dread as we watched him struggle to stand. Even after a few days on the drip, he was still incredibly weak and wobbly, and it was clear he had a long way to go. It was heart-wrenching to see him struggle to walk towards us, his little body shaking with effort, but his determination to be close to us was unmistakable. Despite his physical challenges, Ginge had managed to regain his sight, and the joy in his purring was a testament to his relief and happiness at seeing us again.

But there were still obstacles to overcome. His perception of distance was severely compromised, causing him to misjudge how far away objects were from him. Even something as simple as holding a finger up to his face was a challenge, as he would often crash into it. It was clear he still had a long way to go before he could come home, and we knew that it would take time and patience to help him fully recover. But we were determined to do whatever it took to help our little fighter get back to his old self.

While Ginge did go on to make a good recovery, the neurological damage he suffered from being lost and malnourished was still evident. Though he could now walk with better coordination and had put on some weight, he had a persistent tilt to his head that caused him to lose his balance and fall over. Despite this setback, we were overjoyed to have him back home with us.

Since his ordeal, Ginge had undergone a dramatic shift in personality. Gone was his former independence and wanderlust, which was replaced by a newfound desire to be constantly close to

us. He sought continual affection and would meow until we picked him up and cuddled him, a behaviour that he never displayed prior to his disappearance. He was hesitant to venture outside unless we were with him, and seemed to have developed a fear of wind and rain that left him cowering and meowing in protest. We could only speculate that his time spent lost and exposed to the elements had left him traumatised in some way, and we were determined to give him the love and care he needed to help him heal.

As time progressed, Ginge's head-tilting issue became less severe, and I just picked him up and gave him a cuddle whenever I noticed him doing it. I could see the appreciation in his eyes, as if he knew I was there for him. Despite his neurological condition, he remained a happy and affectionate cat. Perhaps some of us are simply born with an indomitable spirit, and Ginge is a true testament to that. In fact, if you didn't know about his condition, you'd never suspect that anything was wrong with him. He'd spend his days enjoying the simple pleasures of life – lounging in the garden, snuggling up on the sofa, and meowing for ham, his favourite treat.

Watching him live his life to the full was truly inspirational, and I am proud to have been his mum and grateful for every moment we got to spend together.

At the beginning of the Covid-19 pandemic, Ginge's health worsened significantly. His sight weakened, he went completely deaf, and he was clearly frail. When I took him to the vet, due to lockdown restrictions, I had to leave him in the cat carrier outside the vet's office and wait in the car park. They called my mobile to say that it was his time, and there was nothing more they could do for him. I was devastated but, through my tears, I managed to ask the vet and his nurse to give him a kiss on the head and a cuddle before putting him to sleep, and they assured me they

would. Afterwards, they wrapped him in towels, put him back in the carrier and brought him out to my car. Then, from a safe distance, they expressed their condolences and left me alone with my sorrow. I put Ginge in the car and cried my heart out. I'd had him for 17 joyful years.

Even though I'd known this day would come, I was not prepared for the overwhelming sense of loss I felt. Ginge was an exceptional cat who lived a long and happy life, despite the problems he had to overcome. He was deeply loved and cherished by all who knew him.

His glass plaque reads:

You were a true survivor.
R.I.P GINGE X
2003 – 2020

5

🐈 SHREK

Introducing Shrek, the charming ginger and white cat whose unique personality and adorable quirks made him a little star. As the son of our lovely Shakira and brother of Ginge, Shrek had a subtle appearance, with ginger stripes that ran from the top of his head all the way down to his tail, which resembled the rings of a ring-tailed lemur.

While his brothers were busy roughhousing and playing, Shrek was content to snuggle up with his mum and enjoy her company. He was the last of his litter to wean off her, and I suspect this is why he retained his childlike innocence. But even as he got older, he continued to seek out his mother's affection, much to her annoyance.

As a kitten, Shrek was a cautious learner who preferred to observe his brothers before trying anything new. He didn't like being bundled up or playing rough and instead preferred playing with cat toys. His cute habit of chasing his tail never failed to make me smile. He also had a soft spot for snuggling with his brothers, often squeezing his way into the middle of them for a warm nap.

Although he loved to chatter at birds from the safety of the window, Shrek was never much of a hunter, and he never brought

any prey back to the house. He was simply a happy-go-lucky cat who loved to cuddle, play, and chill.

Shrek was undoubtedly a social butterfly, and with his friendly demeanour and loving nature, he was always seeking attention from those around him. However, there were times when his behaviour left us wondering if he was a bit simple. He would often wander around the house headbutting random objects, from table legs to door frames, as if he were auditioning for a role as a battering ram. We could hear the thud of skull as he did so, yet he seemed unbothered by it all. Dave would often quip, "Where there's no sense, there's no feeling," and Shrek's actions certainly supported that saying. This peculiar behaviour continued throughout his entire life, leaving us all mystified, yet amused.

Shrek was a cat who knew how to live life on his own terms. He had this laidback vibe that made you wonder if he walked around in his own little bubble. Nothing seemed to faze him.

At the tender age of three, Shrek still found comfort in cuddling up to his mum on the sofa and following her around. Sometimes she was cool with it, but other times she needed her own space. That didn't stop Shrek, though. He just kept on following her and cuddling up to her until she had enough and hit out at him. It was hilarious to watch him sulk on the sofa and lay there all by himself. Whenever Shrek wasn't bothering his mum, he would come and sit next to me. It was his way of saying, "Hey, I want attention too," but instead of meowing or rubbing against me, he would give me a tiny bite on my hand. It didn't hurt, but it definitely caught me by surprise. That was his way of asking me to stroke him and if he wanted more, he would give me another little bite to let me know. Shrek sure had a funny way of communicating, but it was hard not to love him for it.

Unlike his adventurous brothers, who were always out in the garden, Shrek preferred to explore closer to home. He would wander around but never go too far.

Shrek was a healthy cat who rarely needed to visit the vet, but when he was six years old, he disappeared at the same time as his brother, Ginge. We were devastated and did everything we could to find them, putting up posters and searching high and low. But despite our best efforts, they remained missing for three long months.

Then one day we received a call from a local vet. Someone had found Shrek and taken him there and, thankfully, his microchip led the vet back to his rightful family. We learned that he had been in a town just twenty minutes from our house, where he had found his way into a lady's garden and won her over with his sweet nature. She had named him Georgie and given him a new home, complete with toys, bowls, and a cat post. She had grown so attached to him that she cried when we came to take him back, even though she knew he belonged with us. As we stood in her garden, she called out to him, "Georgie, Georgie," and to our relief, Shrek came running towards us. But when we called out to him, he didn't even recognise us. He seemed confused, distant, and disoriented. We tried to coax him closer, calling his name and hoping that he would remember us, but he didn't budge, just stared at us blankly. I was upset and couldn't help but cry. The lady consoled me and managed to get Shrek into a carrier for us to take home.

Unfortunately, things didn't go as smoothly as we had hoped. Even when we got him back home, he didn't seem to recognise anyone, not even Shakira and his brothers, whom he had always adored. We tried to keep him safe by blocking the cat flap with a cardboard box, but he managed to escape within a few hours. I blamed myself and felt I had let him down. I should have left him with the lady who had cared for him so lovingly. I couldn't bear the thought of never seeing him again. So, I stood outside in the rain, calling his name and hoping that he would come back to me.

It seemed like an eternity had passed, and I had almost given up hope when he finally appeared at the door, bedraggled, and soaked to the bone. He looked up at me with big, sad eyes, and I could tell he had been through so much. I smiled through my tears, relieved that he was back with us.

Over the next few weeks, we worked hard to help Shrek regain his memory and his confidence. We showered him with love and attention, and eventually he returned to his old self. It was an unpredictable journey, but I'm so glad about the way it turned out. Through it all, we learned how much our pets mean to us; they are more than just animals – they are our family. And when they are lost, we must help them find their way home.

Poor Shrek! Despite being a feline superstar, he couldn't escape the dreaded gum disease and had to say goodbye to his teeth. But don't feel sorry for him, because he didn't let that stop him from being his usual charming self. In fact, with only one tooth left, his signature look changed a bit. Sometimes his lone gnasher would stick out of his mouth and sit on his top lip, giving him an adorable snaggletooth grin that melted everyone's hearts. And let's not forget about the bald spot on his furry chin where the lone pearly white sat, creating a unique, tooth-shaped patch that made him even more lovable.

When my daughter was born, Shrek was the only cat who seemed to understand the significance of this new arrival. He would stay close by, vigilant and protective, and his devotion to her only grew stronger with each passing day. Whether she was playing on her jungle gym or sitting in her highchair, Shrek was

always there, watching over her with the utmost care and attention. I remember one particularly precious moment when my daughter was just 18 months old. She was sitting on the floor with Shrek, reading him a book and pointing to the pictures with a big grin on her face. When she got to the page with the picture of a cat, she patted Shrek on the head and said "cat," as if he were one of the characters in the story. It was clear they had a special bond, which would endure as she grew up.

And grow up she did, always with Shrek by her side. He was her willing participant whenever she wanted to play dress up or have a tea party. And even when he knocked over her teddy bear customers, she would just giggle and say, "Oh, Shrek." They had a connection that went beyond words, a shared language of love and affection. When my daughter started school, I worried Shrek might feel lonely without her. But every day when she came home, he was the first to greet her with his usual enthusiasm, rubbing against her legs and purring with joy. It was clear that their bond was unbreakable, and I felt grateful to have such a loyal and loving feline friend in the family.

Shrek was 16 years old when I returned home from work one day and found him lying on the living room floor. As I approached him, he struggled to get up. Confused and scared, I quickly grabbed a cat carrier to take him to the vet, but before I could make it to the door, Shrek ran out of the cat flap and into the garden. I followed him outside, only to find him lying lifeless on the ground just a few feet away. There were no signs of injury, and I could only assume that he had suffered a heart attack or a stroke.

I knelt beside him, tears streaming down my face as I touched his soft fur for the last time. I told him how much I loved him and how much he meant to me. It was so hard to say goodbye to my darling boy. We buried him in the garden, with a love heart stone marking his resting place.

Shrek had lived a long and happy life, but his sudden passing left us all devastated. My daughter picked him a flower to place in the grave, and we said our final goodbyes. We will always remember his adorable quirks, his love for our family, and the joy he brought into our lives. He will be deeply missed but we are grateful for the memories we have of sweet and loving Shrek.

SHREK

His glass plaque reads:

In our hearts forever
R.I.P SHREK X
2003 – 2018

6
ZEUS

Zeus, the magnificent moggy, was a sight to behold. While his brothers, Ginge and Shrek, were shorthaired, Zeus was a Maine Coon in disguise, with a luxuriously fluffy coat that made him look like a feline lion. His long tufts of fur, which protruded from both ears, and his bushy tail made him seem like he was from another world. Even though he was of the same breed as his brothers, he stood out with his unique appearance that made everyone take notice.

As a kitten, Zeus was a curious explorer, always eager to investigate his surroundings. Though he wasn't as daring as his brother Ginge, he still displayed an adventurous spirit. He would often approach a new object with a cautious sniff and then jump back in surprise, only to approach it once more with newfound courage.

Despite his initial shyness, Zeus had a bold and determined side when it came to food. He was the first to be weaned off milk, and the first to try solid cat food. Once he tasted it, he was hooked, and his love for a good meal only grew with age. He was always the first in line at feeding time and would devour his meals with gusto. His nosh-loving personality sometimes led to a comical display of selfishness. He would often lick all the gravy off the meat in his bowl, then move on to the other dishes, leaving none left for our other cats.

To avoid conflict, I switched to jelly-based food instead. I used to joke that if Zeus was ever adopted, his new family might think he was some sort of street cat who'd had to fight for every scrap of food. But really, he just loved his grub, and he wasn't shy about showing it.

Zeus, the foodie feline, had a nose for all things delicious. He was like a furry detective, always on the lookout for any morsel that might accidentally fall in his direction. He would follow you around, hypnotised by the slightest rustle of a crisp packet or the faint sound of the fridge opening, and there was no point trying to open it quietly – Zeus had superhuman hearing that would put even the most advanced spy gadgets to shame.

While his competition (aka the other cats) didn't bother as much with begging, Zeus never gave up hope. Occasionally, we would give in to his charms and treat him to some of his favourite foods. He had a soft spot for boiled eggs and would watch me intently as I prepared one for him. And let's not forget his love for McDonald's fries. Whenever he started begging, all the other cats would come running, thinking they were in for a treat, only to find that it was just Zeus being his usual food-obsessed self. But that didn't stop him from trying, and we couldn't help but laugh at his persistence.

When Zeus wasn't thinking about food, he was happiest out in the garden, basking in the sun or frolicking in the snow. But when it came to rain, well, let's just say he wasn't a fan. It took him ages to get himself cleaned up after getting caught in a downpour, much to the amusement of the other cats. But hey, he knew how to look after himself, and he took great pride in his appearance, grooming himself to perfection. His white fur was always immaculate and spotless, a testament to his diligent self-care routine.

Ah, Zeus, the balloon bandit! In his younger years, he'd disappear for hours and come back with deflated balloons in his mouth – and boy did he love those little bits of rubber. He'd bat them around the living room, swatting them with his paws and chasing them like he was a kitten again. We didn't dare touch his precious haul because Zeus was fiercely protective of it. He'd guard the balloons like a dragon protecting its hoard of treasure. I couldn't help but wonder where the heck he was getting all those balloons from. Was he attending secret cat parties? Breaking into people's homes? Or did he have a secret stash hidden away somewhere? I mean, the mystery remains unsolved!

When my daughter was born, Zeus had no clue what to make of this tiny, squirming creature. The once curious kitten turned into a hesitant and skittish feline, unsure of how to approach this new addition to the family. But as my daughter grew older and started to eat solid foods, Zeus found a newfound appreciation for her. He realised that she was a veritable food factory, and that every mealtime was a chance for him to score some tasty leftovers. The highchair became his new favourite piece of furniture, and he would sit patiently beneath it, ready to hoover up any crumbs that fell from above. My daughter soon caught on and turned feeding time into a game, tossing bits of cucumber and quiche down to her new friend. Though Mummy eventually put a stop to the game, Zeus remained steadfast in his quest for snacks. As my daughter grew older, she learned which scraps Zeus was allowed and took on the role of treat dispenser. From then on, the two became the best of friends.

Zeus's fluffiness got better with time. His giant mane and luxurious tail reminded me of a feather duster on steroids. But though lovely to stroke, there was a downside to his glorious coat – his tail was like a wrecking ball. Every time he walked past the

coffee table, his tail would swipe across it, sending everything on it flying. And the worst part? He would look back with an innocent expression, as if to say, "What was that?"

But that wasn't the only challenge we faced with Zeus's fur. The fur on his tummy used to get matted, and we had to take him to the vet to get it sorted. It wasn't easy trying to brush him, either, as he'd hit the brush and try to bite it, before grabbing it and kicking it with his back legs. He was one strong kitty, and I was grateful I wasn't on the receiving end of his playfulness. Speaking of playfulness, Zeus was a pro at chasing the laser light. He would speed across the room, not even pausing to check if any two-legged beings were in his way. If he ploughed into you, it was just collateral damage – he was on a mission to catch that pesky red dot.

At times, he would climb onto your lap and gaze into your eyes with an affectionate intensity before nuzzling his head against yours. Occasionally, he would even begin to pat your stomach, as if he were playing a tune on a piano. However, due to his hefty size, I often had to redirect his paws away from my vital organs; his piano playing could get a little rough for my liking.

Zeus was undoubtably the leader of the pack. He was always after more food, more attention, and more playtime than his brothers. He didn't care about taking turns or sharing, he was all about getting what he wanted when he wanted it. Despite his selfish streak, he was never aggressive, and he loved attention from anyone who would give it to him.

Oh, and let me tell you about his toys. They were his and no one else's. And if you took a break from your food, well, that was HIS too. But that was all part of his charm. He was a lovable tyrant, and we couldn't help but adore him.

As Zeus hit his golden years, he lost some of his fluffiness and was no longer the giant, majestic cat he once was. Instead, he looked frail and vulnerable and had slimmed down considerably. Despite his physical changes, Zeus still had so much love to give. His gentle head bobbed, and his loving purrs were a constant reminder of the bond we had built over the years. And in his advanced age, he became a true lap cat, always eager to snuggle up for a cuddle. In those quiet moments spent together, I could feel his unconditional love radiating from his little furry body. He may not have been the fluffy, playful kitten that I had first met, but he had grown into a wise and gentle soul.

When he reached the grand old age of 17, Zeus took a turn for the worse. Despite eating plenty, he kept losing weight. The vet prescribed thyroid tablets, which didn't seem to work. We then noticed thick snot coming from one of his nostrils, which medication also didn't improve. The vet suggested further tests to try and determine the underlying issue. However, given his age, I made the difficult decision to end his distress. By then he had become increasingly lethargic, and he spent most of his time sleeping in the litter tray. I could see the tiredness in his eyes, and it broke my heart. Before the vet took him away, I held him close and told him how much I loved him and how much he meant to me. I cried uncontrollably, not wanting to let him go.

I buried him in the garden the next morning, wrapped in a blanket. In the grave alongside him, I placed a balloon containing one puff of air, which was to symbolise his last breath. The silence without him was deafening, something I don't think I will ever get used to.

ZEUS

His glass plaque reads:

We will always remember your fluffy, greedy self.
We will never forget you.
R.I.P ZEUS X
2003 – 2020

7
OOSHEE

As soon as I saw the ad for the grey, striped kitten, I knew I had to have him. My heart skipped a beat as we pulled up to the seller's house, and before I knew it, I was being introduced to the most adorable creature I had ever seen. He had these massive ears that seemed to have a life of their own, a spotty belly and a distinctive M marking on his forehead. But it was his piercing orange eyes that really caught my attention. It was as if they were hypnotising me to take him home.

When I reached down to stroke him, he started meowing, begging me to continue, and oh, that purr! It was so loud and consistent, like a rumbling engine. I knew right there and then that this little guy was coming home with us.

We named him Ooshee, which sounds like the word for ears in Russian. Eventually, our new boy grew into his oversized ears, and although they didn't stand out as much as they did when we first saw him, his name served as a continual, sweet reminder of this adorable early feature.

When Ooshee first came home, he was a bundle of energy and curiosity. He fearlessly approached the other cats and boldly explored his new surroundings. One of his favourite games involved a giant rug in the living room. He would sprint at full speed and dive underneath it, then patiently wait for his next victim to stroll

by. With a flick of his paw, he would then swat at them, watching with delight as they jumped in surprise, often bouncing a foot into the air. With eyes full of mischief, Ooshee could keep this game going for hours. Eventually, though, the other cats caught on and would sneak up on him in revenge.

One of Ooshee's most treasured toys was a soft frog on a stick. When we held it up high, he would jump up and catch it with his tiny paws. But when he wanted to play alone, he would grip the frog tightly in his mouth and proudly walk around with the stick trailing behind him, occasionally whacking it into anything that got in his way. If it ever got stuck, he would tug and pull with all his might until it was free, and then sit next to it and meow until someone came to play again.

As a kitten, Ooshee slept in our room. Before bed, he would play a game that involved pouncing on our hands under the covers. He'd crouch down low, his giant ears pricked, and then launch himself into the air, landing on our hands and playfully biting and kicking at the covers. We would keep playing until he was tired and ready for sleep, but sometimes in the middle of the night, our feet would unknowingly move and Ooshee would pounce again, thinking it was playtime. His bum wiggle was the telltale sign of an impending attack, and our toes would often bear the brunt of his playful wrath.

Ooshee was quite the character and had a penchant for entertaining us with his silly antics. One of his favourite pastimes was to sit on the windowsill and scrape at the window using the pads of his paws. It was as if he was trying to scratch his way out of the house or was working hard to make the glass sparkling clean. It was a hilarious sight to witness, especially if you were outside looking in. He continued this peculiar habit into adulthood. We always wondered what was going through his little feline brain –

perhaps he had dreams of becoming an escape artist or a window cleaner extraordinaire! Either way, he certainly kept us amused with his funny quirks.

Ooshee's athleticism was truly astounding. Thanks to his exceptionally long back legs, he could leap like a feline superhero! One afternoon, while we were enjoying a peaceful garden moment, a pigeon flew low across the lawn, catching the attention of our eagle-eyed Ooshee. In an instant, he sprang into action, launching himself higher than any of our other cats could even dream of. With lightning-fast reflexes, he twisted mid-air, snatched the unsuspecting bird out of the sky and bolted off with it! Dave and I were left gaping in amazement, barely able to process what we had just witnessed.

Ooshee's hatred for car trips was something to behold. It wasn't just a mild dislike; it was a full-blown protest. Even before we got in the car, he knew what was coming and his big, mournful howls could be heard all the way down the street. Once we were on the road, the real drama began. He would dig and scratch at the carrier as if trying to tunnel his way out, and his meows would become louder and more desperate with every passing mile.

But the real kicker was what happened when we finally arrived at the vet's surgery. Despite his protests, Ooshee would inevitably pee and poo in his carrier, as if to make his feelings about the whole ordeal crystal clear. The staff at the surgery were always kind and understanding, though. Before he was seen by the vet, they would take the carrier from us and clean it up, along with Ooshee himself.

And then, like magic, on the journey home, Ooshee would transform. The same cat who had been a howling, scratching, pooping mess on the way to the vet would suddenly become as calm and content as can be, with only a few tiny meows to indicate

he had ever been anything but perfectly well behaved in the car. It was almost as if he was saying, "See? I told you I didn't want to go."

As Ooshee matured, his once dark fur transformed into a lighter hue, and his distinctive stripes became more pronounced and darker. But that wasn't the only thing that changed about him. He developed a meow like no other – it was a long, drawn-out call that sounded like a cross between a Siamese cat and a soprano singer hitting a high note. Whenever he returned from his outdoor adventures, he would announce his arrival with this unique meow, as if to say, "I'm home, everyone."

But that was just the beginning of Ooshee's talking abilities. You could ask him any question, and he would meow back in response, as if he were actually carrying on a conversation with you. And the more questions you asked, the more he would answer. It was like playing a game with a furry little quiz show host.

Of course, Ooshee wasn't the only talkative cat in the household. Ginge also loved to chat, so if you asked them both a question at the same time, you were in for a wild ride of back and forth meowing and playful banter. As their human, you were just a crazy cat lady talking to two feline comedians. But really, who could blame you for indulging in such delightful company?

Ooshee was the ultimate curious cat, and he was always poking his nose where it didn't belong. It didn't matter how many times we caught him sneaking past us into forbidden areas, he would always find a way to explore. The loft was his ultimate adventure playground. We'd often hear him meowing from up there, demanding to be let out. And whenever we forgot to shut the airing cupboard door, Ooshee would be in there like a flash, no doubt looking for some secret kitty hideaway.

But his nosiness could sometimes land him in trouble. Like the time we found him stuck in the shed, looking as guilty as sin.

Or the time he snuck into the garage and got himself trapped. Luckily, we always found a way to get him out. And we made a point of calling out his name before shutting any doors, just in case he was lurking inside.

Ooshee was a natural born hunter, and he stalked birds and mice with incredible focus and determination. He'd bring his latest prey into the house, still alive and kicking, and sit there proudly while I tried to catch it and set it free. I learned to keep him in a separate room during these times, as he'd often try to catch the creature before I could release it, and if he succeeded, he'd run around the house with it in his mouth, like a champion.

One time, he brought in something that managed to escape and hide somewhere in the house. When I came downstairs in the middle of the night, I found Ooshee and all our other cats sitting together, intently staring at the same spot. It was like they were all in on a secret, and I knew right away that I had a rescue mission on my hands.

As he grew older, Ooshee didn't hunt as much, which was a relief for both of us. I remember watching in horror one day as a bird flew into the window while we were both outside. It landed right by Ooshee's feet. Now, in his younger days, Ooshee would have pounced on it before it had even hit the ground, but now he just looked at it before glancing up at me with an expression that seemed to say, "Are you going to do something about that?" I picked up the shocked bird while Ooshee simply went back to sleep, content in his retirement from the hunting life.

One thing that Ooshee absolutely adored throughout his life was the sunshine. He would bask in the warmth of the sun for hours on end, his little spotted belly exposed as he swatted away any passing flies. When he got too hot, he would wander back

inside to cool off, but he always made sure to get his fill of vitamin D first.

Another thing that changed as Ooshee aged was his attitude to laps. In his younger years, Ooshee was a fiercely independent cat, and he wouldn't be caught dead stretching across someone's knees. He had his own agenda and was more than happy to go about his business, thank you very much. However, that didn't mean he wasn't a demanding little guy when he fancied some attention. He knew just how to get what he wanted, and that usually meant incessant meowing and headbutts until you gave in and gave him some love.

But as he got older, something else shifted in Mr Ooshee, besides giving up hunting. Maybe he realised that life was short, or maybe he just wanted a little extra love and affection. Either way, he started to become more of a lap cat, curling up and purring contentedly. And the best part? He seemed to enjoy being kissed on the head and picked up, which was a huge change from his younger days. He would even stretch his little paws up your legs, as if to say, "Pick me up, human," and when you obliged, he would rub his face against yours, purring all the while.

Ooshee's 17th birthday in November 2021 was a bittersweet occasion. Just a year earlier, we had received the devastating news that he had cancer of the stomach and kidneys. As time passed, Ooshee's condition worsened, and he became incontinent. It was heartwrenching to see this once strong feline become so slow. He spent most of his time in his bed, only venturing out for food, but each night he would climb on my lap seeking comfort and warmth. It was a precious moment, but it also served as a reminder of how fleeting life can be. Looking at him, I couldn't help but think of the many years we had spent together, never imagining that he would one day be this old and frail.

As the days went by, Ooshee's exhaustion became more pronounced, and he stopped getting out of bed altogether. It was clear he was no longer happy, and it was time to let him go. The trip to the vet was a silent one, a stark contrast to the many noisy ones we had taken there in the past. When we arrived, Ooshee seemed to understand what was happening. He looked around the room, took a deep breath and lay down on the table as if he were ready for a long rest. The vet agreed it was time to say goodbye and we tearfully said our final farewells.

The loss of Ooshee was devastating, leaving a void in our lives that can never be filled. Losing him was a reminder of the fragility of life, and how we must cherish every moment we have with those we love.

OOSHEE

His glass plaque reads:

A true companion who brought so much warmth and
happiness into my life.
R.I.P OOSHEE X
2004–2022

8
SQUISHY

One day, my friend called me up and exclaimed, "You won't believe it, I've found some cats with thumbs for sale!" At first, I thought she was pulling my leg. But as she continued to describe these little wonders, and I realised she was telling the truth, I couldn't help but burst out laughing at the absurdity of it all. I mean, cats with thumbs. What would be next? Cats that can drive cars or play the piano?

Despite my initial doubts, I couldn't resist the temptation to see these cats for myself. As my friend had agreed in advance to buy a kitten, the breeder had arranged to take the litter over to her house so she could choose one. So, I drove over to hers, half expecting to see a bunch of cats wearing mittens. As soon as I saw my friend, I could tell she was bursting with excitement. She was bouncing up and down like a kid on Christmas morning. And to be fair, I probably would have been the same had I just discovered something so amazing.

"Come on, come on," she practically yelled, grabbing my arm and dragging me over to where the kittens were playing. "You have to see this."

And, boy, was she right. As soon as I caught sight of those little furballs, I knew I was witnessing something truly special. They were like no cats I'd ever seen before – and I've seen a lot of cats in

my time. I couldn't help but stare in wonder. Their little thumbs were sticking out like tiny human digits. It was as if these cats were trying to be human, or maybe they were part of some secret feline revolutionary gang preparing to take over the world.

In any case, I knew that I had to have one of these little thumb-wielding kittens for myself. Who knows, maybe one day they would learn to open doors or use a smartphone.

My friend explained that only two of the six kittens in the litter had this 'abnormality'– although, to be honest, I wasn't sure that I agreed with that assessment. To me, these little kitties were more like little miracles.

She told me that the breeder had assumed nobody would want them because of their unique anatomy, but I knew I couldn't let that happen. I just had to take one of these wonders home with me. Before I even had a chance to think it over, my mouth had already agreed to take on the male kitten. And, honestly, I didn't regret it for a second. These cats were one of a kind, and I knew that I would give this kitten the best possible life – thumbs and all.

As soon as I got the little four-month-old home, my curiosity was piqued. What was the deal with his extra digit? Was it a deformity? Would it affect him as he grew? I decided to go on the internet and delve into the history of polydactyl cats.

The first record of a polydactyl cat dates back to 1868, with the 'polydactyl' originating from the Greek words 'poly' meaning 'many', and 'daktylos' meaning finger or toe.

Cats typically have 18 toes, with five toes on each front paw and four on each hind paw. Polydactyly is a genetic mutation in which a kitten is born with as many as nine digits on their front and/or hind paws, with the condition commonly found on the front paws. It's a dominant gene and an inherited trait, which may explain why the number of polydactyl cats seems to be growing. It's rare for a cat to have polydactyl hind paws only, and polydactyly of all four paws is even less common. My new feline friend had extra digits on all four paws, making him super unique.

The Nobel Prize-winning author Ernest Hemingway was a fan of polydactyl cats, with his home in Key West, Florida, now housing approximately fifty descendants of his cherished pets, about half of which are polydactyl. 'Hemingway cats', as they're sometimes referred to, are just one example of how polydactyl pusses have been adored throughout history.

In the early 20th century, a polydactyl cat even made it to the White House, with President Theodore Roosevelt having a six-toed 'first kitty' called Slipper.

The Guinness World Record holder for the cat with the most toes is Jake, a ginger cat who had an astounding 28 toes, seven on each paw, each with its own claw, pad and bone structure.

Meanwhile, a cat called Lil Bub took the internet by storm with her extreme dwarfism and polydactyly on all four paws.

But back to my own kitten. Let's start with his name – Squishy. It was inspired by Dory's loveable character in *Finding Nemo*, as she affectionately calls her new friend, a jellyfish, 'Squishy'. When I first saw my new furry companion, I knew instantly that he would be *my* Squishy.

Squishy's unique physical trait of having extra toes on each paw made him stand out in a crowd. When I took him to the vet for his first check-up, even the professionals were amazed as they had never seen a polydactyl cat in real life. Everyone at the clinic wanted a closer look, and he lapped up all the attention, basking in the love and admiration. Squishy's fur was a gorgeous strawberry blonde shade, with a full white chest and neck that made him look even more unique and adorable.

But as he grew up, Squishy became more enamoured with the company of cats than humans. Although not particularly a people person, Squishy still had his admirers, and he loved to sit in his favourite spot, on top of my car, and watch the world go by. The posties and delivery people who came to our door were always surprised to see his extra toes and would often stop to pet him. While he tolerated their attention, Squishy wasn't one for over-the-top displays of affection.

As a kitten, Squishy displayed his rebellious side by flipping over his cat bed and taking naps underneath it. You could always find him by looking for his adorable tail sticking out. But it would be unwise to let his cute appearance fool you. Squishy had a strict five-second policy when it came to cuddles. Basically, you had to put him down before you finished counting to five, otherwise he would play merry hell. It's like he was saying, "I love you, human, but not that much."

And while most cats meow or purr loudly to get attention, Squishy preferred to keep it low key. He had a quiet purr that sounded more like a chirp.

Squishy's best bud was Ooshee. Those two would run all over the house chasing each other like crazy and then head outside to continue the party. They'd be out for hours hunting and sunbathing, and when Ooshee finally decided he'd had enough, Squishy was content to chill out on his own.

Squishy was like the king of his castle, ruling over his domain with the grace of a feline monarch. He would lounge in the garden with his legs stretched out like a spinx, his tail flicked over to one side, surveying his territory with a look of regal satisfaction. We even built him his own cat house, complete with a carpeted interior walkway and a sleeping shelf fit for a king. But despite his royal status, he was a low-maintenance kitty who didn't need much fussing over. He didn't care what we were up to or what treats were on offer, but on the rare occasion he did feel like some attention, he would saunter over, enjoy a brief stroke and then go back to ruling his kingdom. Once, we even caught him sitting on the scratchy post gazing at his own photo. He was lost in his own image, like a true king. And let's be honest, with those adorable little thumbs and majestic posture, who could blame him for being so vain? All hail King Squishy, ruler of all things feline and fabulous!

Squishy's love for snow was something truly magical. As soon as a few flakes started to fall from the sky, he would be outside, gazing up at the winter wonderland that had descended upon his domain. With his little paws padding softly through the snow, he would try and catch the snowflakes in his mouth, his eyes sparkling with excitement. And when I threw snowballs his way, he bounded after them with all the energy and enthusiasm of a kitten. Watching Squishy play in the snow was like watching a work of art come to life. He was a masterpiece in motion.

One day, Squishy came home with a monstrous abscess on the side of his face. It was clear that he had been in a nasty brawl with another cat. Despite his usually gentle demeanour, it seemed that Squishy was not one to back down from a challenge. We rushed him to the vet, who quickly got to work shaving his fur and draining the abscess. The vet recommended that he be kept indoors to allow his wounds to heal properly. Squishy was not happy about this, as he was used to spending his days exploring and soaking up the sun. But we knew it was for his own good, and we did our best to keep him entertained and comfortable during his recovery.

After a few weeks, Squishy's wound had healed, and he

was ready to take on the world once again. But this time with a newfound sense of caution and a greater appreciation for the comfort and safety of his home.

Squishy lived a long and happy life, to the age of 15, but towards the end it was clear that his body was starting to give up on him. He seemed to have lost his playful spirit. Even his purr/chirp was barely audible.

One wet and miserable day, I found Squishy sitting outside in the garden, rain pouring down on him. I immediately brought him inside, but he didn't show any interest in food or water. He just sat in the corner, his paws tucked under him, looking tired and defeated. I took him to the vet, but Squishy remained motionless in the corner of his carrier. He didn't even flinch when the vet examined him. It was as if he had already accepted his fate. The vet said it was time, and that Squishy had lived a good life and deserved to go peacefully. And so, with a heavy heart, I said goodbye to my dear old friend.

It's never easy to let go of someone you love, and Squishy was no exception. He was more than just a pet; he was a beloved member of our family. His gentle nature, his quiet presence and his unconditional love will be deeply missed.

His glass plaque reads:

You will always be our little sun worshipper.
R.I.P SQUISHY X
2006 – 2021

9

SUSHI

One ordinary day, I was going about my usual routine when a shocking piece of information came to my attention. A friend mentioned that a woman she knew had recently purchased a precious kitten, only to decide she no longer wanted it after having a baby. Apparently, she claimed she no longer had time for the kitten and threatened to abandon it outside in the cold, shutting the door on it forever. My heart sank at the thought of this helpless little creature being left to fend for itself. So, I asked for the woman's contact details and paid her a visit.

Upon arriving at her house, the lady reiterated the same story I had heard earlier. She confessed that the kitten had become too much of a commitment for her. The kitten, a sweet and friendly female tabby, seemed to be in good health, and my heart went out to her. Without a second thought, I made the decision to take her into my care and took her to the cat carrier I kept in my car. Before departing, I suggested to the woman that she refrain from acquiring any more animals in the future.

It's a sad truth that some people don't understand the lifelong commitment that comes with owning a pet. The idea of taking on a new furry companion might seem exciting at first, but when the novelty wears off, some people are quick to dispose of their animals. It's a notion that I can never wrap my head around. In my opinion, owning a pet should come with a licence, and those who mistreat them should be banned from owning animals for life. After all, our pets rely solely on us for their wellbeing, and we should never take that responsibility lightly.

I named the cat Sushi, and as soon as I brought her home, it was clear that she was a bundle of joy and happiness. She eagerly explored every corner of the house, purring loudly and playfully pouncing on anything in her path. However, as I sat with her on the sofa, admiring her cuteness, I noticed a flea crawling on her face. Concerned, I decided to give her a thorough check over with a flea comb.

To my horror, I quickly discovered that Sushi was covered in fleas. I'm not talking a few of the little mites here and there, but an overwhelming infestation that had invaded every inch of her tiny body. It was evident that this poor kitten had been suffering for quite some time. I set about defleaing her and providing her with some much-needed relief. I carefully combed through her fur, ensuring I dipped the comb into a bowl of boiling water to kill the fleas before plunging it into cold water to cool it down. To my surprise, Sushi sat patiently through the entire process, enjoying every bit of the attention and care. It took a good hour to fully rid her of the fleas, but I could tell she felt much better for it.

My new kitty was blessed with a stunning, grey-striped coat, with bright white patches on her chin, tummy and paws. Her eyes were hypnotic green, and they lit up whenever she purred. Despite her rocky start to life, she soon blossomed into a cherished member of our family.

Sushi's playful spirit was contagious, and we loved watching her entertain herself with her favourite green plastic ball. She had a unique way of playing with it, grabbing onto the feathers that jutted out from the top with her mouth and prancing around the house, showing off her new prize. It was a joy to see her so happy and carefree. She'd chase after the ball and drop it, only to repeat the game over and over again.

But Sushi had her boundaries, and one of them centred on her belly. She made it clear with her quick paws and sharp teeth that belly rubs were off-limits. However, as she grew older, she surprised us by lying on her back and inviting us to rub her tummy. We were hesitant at first, but she looked so adorable we couldn't resist. To our amazement, she didn't attack us, but instead purred contently. It was a confusing turn of events, but we chalked it up to Sushi mellowing with age and learning to trust us even more.

Sushi's obsession with drinking water started when she was a kitten. Her main mission in life has always been to slurp from any vessel containing water, including glasses left on the kitchen counter, puddles, and even buckets. She is always up for a drink. Even now, we have to keep a close eye on our water bottles in case she sticks her tongue in them. At first, we were worried about her excessive drinking, but our vet reassured us that she is perfectly healthy. So, to satisfy her thirst, we decided to purchase two water features – one for indoors and one for outside. The indoor fountain mimics the sensation of drinking from a tap, which Sushi absolutely adores, although we often have to clear up after her as she also likes to scoop the water onto the floor.

Sushi is a lap cat through and through, but she is not one for sharing. Whenever she's on my knee, she'll shoot death glares at any of the other cats who dare approach. They quickly shrink away in fear, and I can't blame them for feeling intimidated – Sushi's stare could make even the bravest of souls cower in fear! Luckily, a gentle "no" from me is usually enough to calm her down and let the others join us. Once everyone is settled in, Sushi is content so long as she has her preferred spot. Should another cat beat her to my lap (take her spot), Sushi will climb even higher up on me and stick her derrière in her rival's face – she is quite the diva! If I encourage her to move, she huffs and puffs and gives me the most disdainful meow you can imagine.

One thing I've learned about Sushi over the years is that she has a unique character, with her own set of quirks and preferences. For example, she is not keen on having the top of her bottom touched. Most cats don't mind a good stroke from head to tail, but Sushi is different. You have to start from her head, go down her back, and then carefully avoid her sensitive spot before reaching her tail. If you don't follow her rules, you'll quickly find yourself on the receiving end of a bite or scratch.

With her round and plump figure, Sushi exudes confidence and attitude. She is the queen of the neighbourhood, and woe betide any human or animal that forgets it. Even when confronted by a barking dog, she remains calm and collected. One day, she finally had enough of the constant noise coming from one of our neighbour's pooches and decided to take matters into her own paws. She silenced him with a swift smack to the mouth before remaining on the spot and staring him down. When he resumed barking, she launched into an impressive display of left and right paw punches, hitting nothing but air. The dog was stunned into silence. Another time, the same dog tried to chase her along a fence and barked and jumped up at her. Not to be tormented, Sushi stood her ground and began hitting the much bigger dog every time he jumped up. Eventually, he got bored and walked away. Her actions might not make her popular with her canine neighbours, but who can blame her for wanting to be top dog or, in this case, top cat?

One afternoon, I noticed something was off with Sushi. She kept incessantly licking her tummy, and my mind immediately went to the worst-case scenario: fleas. I quickly combed through her fur but found nothing. Still, she kept licking, and I knew something was up. Upon closer inspection, I realised this was far worse than fleas, and my blood ran cold. Sushi had somehow been sliced straight down the middle of her body, exposing her tummy fat. How she managed to do this was beyond me, but there wasn't a single trace of blood anywhere. I rushed her to the vet, and they were equally puzzled by her calm demeanour in the face of such a severe injury. It turned out that she had sliced through her skin, and only the final layer was keeping her internal organs from spilling out. The vet guessed that she'd caught herself on a nail or piece of glass while jumping down from a high spot, but we'll never know exactly what happened. Sushi had to undergo surgery, and we anxiously waited at home for news on her condition. Thankfully, the vet soon called to say that she had pulled through and was going to be OK.

Despite the terrifying experience, Sushi healed remarkably well and eventually was able to walk around and have cuddles again. It was a scary moment, but I'm grateful she received the medical attention she needed and made a full recovery.

In our household, carrier bags and boxes are a constant source of entertainment for our cats, but it's Sushi who really puts them to the test. There's a saying among cat people that goes, "If it fits, I sits," and Sushi embodies this perfectly. In her younger years especially, she'd stick her head into the tiniest of boxes, clearly pondering whether it was possible to fit her whole body inside. If she failed, she'd gracefully climb on top of it. Once, my daughter decided to make a cat house out of a huge box, complete with pink wrapping paper, cat stickers, windows, a door and even a tunnel with a cat flap. The cats were ecstatic, but Sushi was the first one to explore it, of course. As she approached her mature years, Sushi became more discerning with her cardboard box choices, and a few years ago we got her a cat tunnel that she absolutely adores. Whenever she isn't curled up on my lap, I can be sure she is cosily napping in her beloved tunnel.

In February 2020, my world stopped turning when I found Sushi gasping for air. She was 14 years old and had never experienced any breathing problems before. Frantic with worry, I took her to the vet, who quickly diagnosed asthma and rushed her off to an oxygen tent for the night. I was left with so many questions. How could my precious Sushi have developed asthma out of the blue? The vet gave her medication, and I was told to keep a close eye on her breathing and bring her back if it worsened. I followed the vet's instructions to a tee, and thankfully Sushi didn't have any further attacks.

Update 2024

At the age of 17, Sushi developed a small, raspy cough, which prompted multiple visits to the vet in the hopes of identifying its cause. However, without the aid of scans or X-rays, getting a diagnosis proved challenging. Given her advanced age, I was wary of subjecting her to unnecessary stress. Over the course of two weeks, the cough worsened, its raspiness intensifying with each breath. As her 18th birthday approached, I harboured the hope she would defy the odds, but deep down, I knew she was reaching the end of her life. Though her mind remained sharp, her body was showing signs of frailty.

One evening, she seemed bothered by something in her throat and was pawing at her mouth and gagging. After this settled down, I saw that she was generally struggling to breathe. It was a terrifying ordeal, as she had never exhibited such behaviour before. The

car ride to the vet was fraught with anxiety as she repeated the distressing episode. During her examination, the vet noted how much weight she'd lost, as well as the decline in her condition. As Sushi lay on the scales, her fatigue evident in her eyes, I felt she was silently communicating to me that her time had come.

In our final moments together, I poured out my heart to her, expressing my gratitude for her unwavering loyalty and recounting the cherished moments we shared. My tears flowed freely as I whispered my love for her, her purrs offering a bittersweet soundtrack to our farewell. With a heavy heart, I bid her goodbye, promising to hold her memory forever.

She was laid to rest alongside her siblings in the garden, swathed in her beloved pink blanket, with added bluebells and dandelions to demonstrate the beauty she brought into our lives.

SUSHI

Her glass plaque reads:

You were feisty, deeply loved and aged gracefully all the way to the end.
You will be missed so much.
R.I.P SUSHI X
2006 – 2024

10

KOSHKA

The atmosphere was charged with excitement as we embarked on our mission to add a new member to our growing feline family. With nine cats already ruling the roost, we were ready to welcome number ten, and we were filled with anticipation as we set out on our quest to find the perfect addition to our clan.

We headed over to the breeder's house, where we were met with the sight of six adorable kittens, all cuddled up together in a fluffy bundle and sound asleep. As we carefully separated them to get a closer look, we discovered a hidden gem at the bottom of the bundle. Despite being buried under the snoozing pile, she was sound asleep on her back, belly up. The first thing I noticed about her was her stunning, fluffy black and white coat and the long tufts of fur that peeked out from her ears. When the light hit her fur just right, you could see her gorgeous ginger highlights. And her legs were a sight to behold. Her right front leg was white, while her left one was black and white. The pattern was repeated on her back legs but the other way round, giving the impression she had put on mismatched socks. We were immediately smitten and knew she was the one.

Once we got her home, we spent hours trying to come up with the perfect name for our new furry friend, but nothing seemed

quite right. Then my best friend Angel came over and told us the Russian word for cat is Koshka. It's such a unique name that we all instantly fell in love with it. And so Koshka joined our ever-growing family, bringing with her a sense of wonder and delight that only cats can provide.

It was soon clear that Koshka was a unique feline, with a gentle spirit and a heart full of love. She wasn't bold and adventurous like the other cats but rather quiet and cautious, preferring the comfort of a familiar environment to the excitement of the unknown. Loud noises and new people made her nervous, and it took her a while to warm up to strangers.

When our daughter was born, Koshka was understandably wary. The noise and commotion that comes with having a newborn was overwhelming for her, and she kept her distance, observing matters from afar. But Koshka's love for me was unwavering, and over time, she trusted me to introduce her to my daughter. Slowly but surely, she started to warm to our little one, cautiously approaching her for a sniff or a gentle nuzzle.

It was heart-warming to see Koshka's relationship with our daughter evolve over the years. As she matured, she would eagerly seek her out for a cuddle or a stroke, and it brought me immeasurable joy to see the bond that developed between them. It's a testament to the power of love and patience, and a reminder that even the most timid of souls can find courage when surrounded by the warmth and love of a family.

Koshka had a playful spirit that was hard to resist, and there was one toy in particular that really caught her fancy – a carrot on a stick made of soft fabric. She was a natural born hunter, crouching down with her bum in the air and her ears pinned back as she waited for the perfect time to pounce. It was clear that this

toy held a special place in her heart, and no other plaything could compare to the joy it brought her. But there was a more everyday item that Koshka found equally irresistible: the sound of a plastic carrier bag. Whenever someone walked by with one, she would dart after them, jumping up and trying to catch the bag mid-air. It was hilarious to watch her playfully swatting at it with her paws.

Along with her playful nature, Koshka was also a bit of a clean freak. She loved being brushed and would rub her face against the bristles, as if to say, "I can do it, let me show you." The white parts of her fur were always spotlessly clean, and she took great pride in keeping herself groomed to perfection.

Every night was special with Koshka by our side. She had her own spot on the bed – right next to me, with her head on my pillow and her body tucked snugly under the covers. As we bedded down, her loud purring would lull us into a peaceful slumber. But the moment anyone dared to move, even the slightest bit, Koshka's purr would start up again, keeping us awake and on high alert. One of my favourite moments was before we all settled down to sleep, when Koshka was invariably sitting on the bed giving herself a thorough wash. For a bit of fun, I would start to scratch under the covers, which would instantly trigger Koshka's inner predator. She'd pounce on the lump my hand made, her head down, her ears back, her eyes wide with excitement. It was wonderful to watch this fluffy ball of fur in high-alert mode and fully engaged in playtime.

When Koshka was a kitten, she also loved to pounce on toes, behaving towards them as someone would their arch enemy. It didn't matter if you were sitting on the sofa, walking around the house, or even trying to sleep, your toes were fair game. One minute you'd be peacefully watching TV, the next you'd have a furry ball hanging off your tootsies. And the worst part? She never gave up. It's a good thing the novelty wore off as Koshka got older, otherwise we'd all be walking around with battle scars on our feet.

Another of her kittenhood habits involved launching herself at us with all the energy she could muster. She'd spring up from the ground, her tiny paws outstretched, and land on our trousers like a furry missile. Then, using her tiny claws as grappling hooks, she'd scrabble her way up to our stomachs, leaving a trail of tiny puncture holes in her wake. But despite the scratches, we couldn't resist giving her a snuggle – her soft fur and adorable little face made it all worth it.

Koshka had a peculiar fascination that set her apart from our other felines. Whenever we were using the toilet, she'd creep up beside us and wait patiently, like an ever-loyal companion. But it wasn't our company that she was after. Her true interest lay in the water that swished around in the bowl. As soon as we were finished and ready to flush, Koshka would leap up onto the toilet seat and stare down into the swirling vortex. She was utterly transfixed by the mesmerising dance of the water, her eyes locked onto the hypnotic motion. To her, it must have been like looking at a magical portal into another dimension. It's hard to say what went through her mind when she saw it, but one thing's for sure – Koshka was not your ordinary cat!

Koshka was also a master at the art of napping, and as a kitten, she would curl up into the most adorable positions that would make your heart melt. I'd catch her sleeping in the funniest of ways, from upside down to contorted into a ball. We used to play a game we called '3-2-1', where we would count down and see how quickly she could drift off into a peaceful slumber. It never took long for her to succumb to a blissful dreamworld.

As she loved sleeping so much, we got her a doughnut-shaped bed that was big enough for her to stretch out and relax in. But little did we know that Koshka had other plans. As soon as we placed the bed in the living room, she rushed over to it, flopped onto her side, and began manoeuvring herself round the edge while still lying on the floor. The bed spun around and around, with Koshka looking like a tiny racing car driver taking laps around a giant doughnut racetrack. She had a blast, and went on to spend hours playing, and then lounging, in her new favourite bed.

In the quiet of the evening, when the day had tired her out, Koshka would find her way to the back of the sofa. With a graceful step, she would make her way down to my shoulders and wrap herself around my neck like a cosy scarf. The weight of her little body was incredibly comforting, and the sound of her purr would lull me into a peaceful state. Even though her purr was louder than a lawnmower, I didn't mind because it was a reminder of her love and trust. I would turn up the volume of the TV, and her warm puffs of air would tickle my face as she purred rhythmically. It was a moment that always made me feel contented and loved.

Koshka's red dot obsession was legendary. She'd go wild when she saw it, stalking it like a lioness on the savannah. She'd leap up doors, dart up walls, and even bound up the stairs in a frenzy, all in pursuit of that elusive dot. And the best part was her silly little ear movements. Whenever the dot got too close, she'd flatten them down like a secret ninja cat on a mission. But the moment I'd move it away, they'd pop back up like little periscopes on the hunt. And that bum wiggle! Oh, it was priceless. She'd wind up her little butt like a coiled spring, getting ready for the 'big attack' – only to pounce on the dot with the force of a feather. But my absolute favourite part was the look on her face when the dot disappeared.

She'd sniff around, her eyes darting to the walls as she tried to figure out where it had gone. And when it reappeared on the wall, she'd race over to it like a kid on Christmas morning. It was pure joy to watch.

At first, Koshka was hesitant about venturing into the great outdoors. Even a gust of wind would send her scurrying back inside. But as she grew more courageous, she started exploring further. While the other cats were content to do their business in the garden, Koshka preferred to venture out to the field, seeking solitude and privacy in her moments of need. Once she was done, she'd sprint back across the field, bursting with pride at her little adventure.

As Koshka grew older, she became more selective about who she would interact with. It would take her time to warm up to someone, and until then she would observe them closely, only approaching with a purr and an open invitation to be stroked once she felt 100% comfortable.

Strangely, she also stopped wrapping herself around my neck like a scarf and took to sitting on the back of the sofa, from where she could paw and nibble at my hair.

As someone who has lived with numerous cats, I have learned that boxes are a universal favourite among felines. Koshka was no exception, but she liked to have her own box to play, sleep and hide in. She was not one for sharing her space, and nor did she welcome being disturbed while in it. However, when she did want a cuddle, she would be fiercely affectionate and loving. Although she didn't spend a lot of time outdoors, come the autumn, she loved nothing more than chasing the fallen leaves around the garden and having a mad five minutes of play. The other cats all watched her, but they

never got involved, sensing that this was Koshka's special moment of joy.

In November 2022, Koshka was sadly diagnosed with a tumour in her bladder. We did everything we could to make her comfortable and pain-free, giving her medication every evening in the form of a delicious yoghurt treat, which she adored. If we hadn't given it to her by 6pm, she would gently remind us with some pawing and meows.

Although she spent less time outdoors and lost a few teeth, Koshka still looked incredible for her age, and her loving nature shone through. We cherished every moment with her and showered her with extra special attention, knowing how every minute of love counted now more than ever.

Regrettably, in June 2023, Koshka's condition took a distressing turn. One morning, an unexpected shift occurred when she opted to remain nestled in her bed, bypassing her usual and enthusiastic breakfast routine. I tended to the other cats and then settled beside her, a feeling of concern washing over me. Although her purrs seemed as robust as ever, her reluctance to rise was unsettling. I granted her the space she needed to rest, hoping that time might restore her energy. However, as the hours progressed and dinner time arrived, Koshka's demeanour remained unchanged. Faced with this disconcerting situation, I made the call to seek professional guidance. With the upmost care, I lifted her into her cat carrier and drove her to the vet.

The vet administered an anti-sickness injection in a bid to alleviate her discomfort. Then he sombrely informed us that should Koshka's appetite fail to return over the upcoming days, a heart-wrenching farewell might be the only option. The medication that held the promise of healing would fail to work if she didn't start eating again. With each passing day, I embarked on a quest to rekindle her appetite, offering her myriad delectable treats in a bid to lure her back to sustenance. Stubbornly, she declined each offering, her unwavering purr serving as a testament to her enduring spirit.

When I realised that Koshka wasn't going to get better, I nestled by her side, embracing her, and praising her incredible nature in whispers. The next day was filled with deep reflection and an overwhelming sense of sadness. Despite my desperate wishes, the heavy burden of responsibility and empathy intertwined and led to an excruciating decision. With a heavy heart, I mustered the strength to say a final goodbye to my Koshka. In doing so, I released her from the grip of suffering. She was a feline of unmatched elegance, and she radiated beauty. Her absence left behind an immense emptiness in my heart. The pain of her passing continues to linger, a poignant reminder of the profound connection we shared and the love that bound us together.

Her glass plaque reads:

One of a kind who will never be forgotten.
R.I.P Koshka xx
2009 – 2023

11
FAREWELL TO THE TEN

With Sushi passing, the era of the famous 10 cats ended, leaving behind a palpable sense of loss in our once bustling household. Though three cats remain, they are of a new generation and untouched by the vibrant chaos of their predecessors. They will never know the camaraderie of our vast family, nor the depth of love that bound us together. All that now remains of my 10 furry companions are snapshots of their time with me. The memories of their quirks and personalities are etched deep in my heart.

I'll never forget Isis, who was always cosying up inches from my face, her purring a symphony of comfort. Then there was Shush, who would leap into my arms for an embrace, filling the air with unconditional affection. Shakira's playful swipes through the banisters were a reminder of the joy of spontaneity. Meanwhile, Ginge's vocal responses during our 'conversations' were a testament to the depth of our connection.

Each memory is a treasure, like Shrek's tender nibbles, a silent plea for affection, or Zeus's incessant demands whenever the fridge door opened. Ooshee's affectionate headbutts were a simple but profound declaration of love. Squishy's unique purr as a door was opened for him was a small gesture brimming with gratitude. I'll remember how, with a gentle tug, Sushi would pull my hand closer, seeking solace in a shared moment of rest. And finally,

I'll remember the playful antics of Koshka, including how she softly chewed my hair. She made a perfect companion for quieter moments.

Maybe one day I'll see glimmers of the 10 in other cats I meet, and if I do, it'll bring back a flood of feelings, making the present feel bold and beautiful once more.

I hope my memories touch your heart, just as they've touched mine. Because in these shared experiences, we find comfort, connection and learn the enduring power of love.

12
WINTER

AKA Aka Do Di Do Di Do Di

It was my daughter's fourth birthday, and, despite our best efforts, she was still holding onto her dummy. When she asked for a kitten for Christmas, I saw an opportunity to gently persuade her to give it up. I promised her that Santa would bring her a kitten, but only if she gave up her dummy. As I suspected, she was immediately on board. And as luck would have it, a woman I worked with, Louise, had a litter of Ragdoll kittens that would be ready for new homes around Christmas time. Excited to learn more about this breed, I did some research and discovered some fascinating facts about these particularly furry felines.

Ragdolls are known for being incredibly friendly and patient, making them perfect companions for children. Their soft and fluffy fur is often compared to that of a rabbit, and they are also known for their piercing blue eyes. They tend to be lap cats and often like to follow their owners around. Interestingly, Ragdolls do not have an undercoat, which sets them apart from other cat breeds. But the most bizarre fact I discovered in relation to Ragdolls was the existence of Janus cats. This is the name for cats who are born with a rare congenital deformity that causes them to have two faces. Back in 1999, in Massachusetts, America, veterinary nurse Marty Stevens adopted a Ragdoll Janus cat whom she named Frankenlouie. He wasn't expected to survive more than a few days, but incredibly went on to live for 15 years. In 2012, *Guinness World Records* recognised Frankenlouie (also known as Frank and Louie) as the world's oldest Janus cat.

After learning all about Ragdolls, it was time for my daughter to meet the litter of kittens. I took her to visit my colleague, who had six, pure-white Ragdolls. To tell them apart, each kitten had a different-coloured collar. My daughter was particularly drawn to a female one with a green collar, who had been temporarily named Greenie. She was the only one who sat on her lap. After that, we made regular visits to watch the kittens grow. We also met the kittens' parents, Bailey and Luna, who were both Ragdolls with distinct personalities and appearances. Amid all this excitement, my daughter still had no inkling that Greenie was her Christmas present, but I knew she was in for a wonderful surprise.

On Christmas Eve, Louise surprised us by bringing Greenie over. Holding the furry ball in her arms, she told my daughter that Father Christmas had sent her a special gift. It was a priceless moment, and my daughter was over the moon with joy. From then on, the kitten, whom we named Winter, quickly became a cherished member of our family. She was a playful cat, and she and my daughter had an instant connection. She loved sleeping next to us during the day and curling up in my daughter's bedroom at night, where she would often rest her head on the pillow and doze off. And when my friends came over, they couldn't resist Winter's stunning blue eyes and captivating appearance. While Winter wasn't a troublemaker, she did have a mischievous side. As a kitten, she liked to nibble on books, and my daughter would often find her gnawing on one while they were trying to read together. Winter also loved trying to catch the tails of our older cats, though she quickly learned that this wasn't a game they were interested in playing. Perhaps one of Winter's quirkiest habits was her love of chewing Sellotape off cardboard boxes. Although we didn't let her continue this pastime, it always made us wonder what was going through her little head.

It's tradition in our household to keep all our kittens close and safe by allowing them to sleep in our bedroom every night, until they turn one. But our feline friend Winter was different. At just six months old, she had already outgrown the cosy comfort of our bedroom and was itching to explore the downstairs with the older cats. At first, I was a bit hesitant to let her go, but her persistent mews and determined scratching at the door finally convinced me. And to my surprise, Winter fitted right in with the other cats. Every morning, I would find her snuggled up in a cat bed with either Ginge or Zeus, completely content and happy. It was lovely to see how quickly she had made herself at home with the senior felines.

For the following year's Christmas present, we got my daughter a doll's house and, after hours of playtime, Winter, ever the curious cat, decided to climb up to the top floor and take a nap. My daughter found it absolutely hilarious that a *Ragdoll* was sleeping in the *doll's* house. I couldn't help but chuckle at the sight of our furry little intruder, who seemed quite content with her new digs. Who knew we had a real-life feline Barbie?

When we had Winter neutered, it had the unexpected side effect of transforming her image. Before the procedure, she was a creamy white ball of fluff, but after the operation, something magical happened. The spot the vet had shaved in preparation to do the op grew back as a perfect square – and in dark grey! It was as if a tiny patch of dark paint had been slapped on her body. Her face, ears, tail and paws were also dark grey, so the colour oddly blended in. I couldn't help but wonder if Winter was going to have this trendy grey square forever. But as she grew and became even

fluffier, the colour of her fur evened out again. Ah, the wonders of a cat's life.

Winter, who we still have now, is certainly a character. She has her own opinion, and she isn't afraid to show it. While they say Ragdolls are the friendliest cat breeds out there, Winter seems to have other ideas. Don't get me wrong, she absolutely adores the human child in the house – they are practically inseparable. But me? Not so much. It's not like I haven't tried to win her over. I've brought her up the same way I have my other cats, but she just doesn't seem to have any interest in me. When I stroke her, she doesn't purr like she does for my daughter. Sometimes, she even licks the spot I touched, like she's trying to get rid of my scent. And if I tell her "no" or try to get her to come down from somewhere, she just ignores me. Maybe it's because I'm the one who takes away her prey when she brings it inside, or maybe it's just that she sees my daughter as her true mother figure. Whatever the reason, I'm clearly not the favourite human in her life.

There is only one time when I'm truly of interest to Winter. Something peculiar happens to her when I'm in the shower. While I'm performing my ablutions, my daughter sometimes brings her up to my bedroom, and if I come through wrapped in a towel and lay on my bed, Winter's personality completely transforms. She becomes incredibly affectionate towards me, purring loudly, nuzzling into me and sitting on top of me. It's as if the water has triggered something in her, turning her into a loving kitten once again. I can't quite figure out why my freshly showered self has this effect on her – anyone would think I had washed using catnip!

Winter and I also share a smidgen of common ground when it comes to the outdoor life. I know they say Ragdolls are naturally indoor cats and shouldn't be allowed to go outside of the home, but I'm of the opinion that no feline is naturally streetwise –

they all have to learn somehow. I kept her in for the first year, but following some consistent meowing and pacing at the patio door, I finally gave in and let her outside. And let me tell you, she was in heaven. She jumped up to catch flies, sniffed the flowers and explored every nook and cranny of the garden – she was one happy cat. And I was happy knowing I'd made the right decision.

But calling her in can be a problem, as Winter doesn't respond to her name. Instead, my daughter started saying, "Do Di Do Di Do Di, come here," and Winter came running. So now every morning, my daughter calls out, "Do Di Do Di Do Di, come and get your breakfast," and Winter responds accordingly. I still just call her Winter, but maybe that's why she doesn't listen to me, and my daughter is her chosen person.

One sunny afternoon, Dave and my daughter attended a fun day organised by an animal welfare charity. Unfortunately, I had to go to work and couldn't join them. They had a virtual cat show, where the animals were to be judged on a photograph rather than a real-life appearance. Of course, we entered photos of all our cats and put them into different categories. My daughter had a blast at the event, and later that day, they announced the winners of the photo contest.

You wouldn't believe it, but Winter won the title of Prettiest Queen and Best in Show. She won a certificate and a huge hamper full of goodies, including a blanket, a cat bed, treats and toys. My daughter was over the moon and so proud of her amazing feline friend. She even came to my office to show me the hamper, which was almost as big as she was. She then rushed home to tell Winter how proud she was of her and display the certificate on the kitchen wall for everyone to see.

Let me tell you about the most p-awesome birthday celebration we had for Winter. For her second birthday, my daughter wanted to make her feel extra special, so she decided to throw her a party. We brainstormed different ideas, but nothing seemed quite as fitting as a birthday cake. Obviously, we couldn't give her an M&S Colin the Caterpillar, so we put our creative hats on and came up with something purr-fectly unique.

First, we got our paws on some Purina Gourmet Gold Melting Heart cat food, which is round and resembles a mini cat cake. We turned it out onto a plate and decorated it with some Webbox Tasty Stick treats, which we broke up to resemble candles. And finally, to add some further flair, we decorated around the cake with wafer-thin ham. My daughter presented the cake to Winter while singing a heartfelt rendition of *Happy Birthday to You*. Winter was ecstatic and eagerly dove in, devouring every morsel of her special treat. It was a joy to watch her enjoying her birthday meal, and we were all so happy to celebrate with her.

When she's not celebrating with cake, Winter's absolute favourite thing to do is hunt; she is a true huntress and can be gone for hours prowling and seeking her next prey. You never know what she will bring home: sometimes it's birds, sometimes it's mice, and sometimes she even manages to catch both in one day. You can see the pride on her face as she walks into the house, meowing triumphantly and dropping her catch onto the floor.

But Winter's not just a fierce hunter, she is also a nosey parker. One day, I came home to find her trapped in my neighbour's car. She was sitting on the passenger seat, looking up at the window with her paws up and meowing for help. I quickly knocked on my neighbour's door and asked him to let her out. He had no idea she was in there and was taken completely by surprise. Winter, on the other hand, walked out nonchalantly as if nothing had happened. She's a drama queen and diva all rolled into one.

At five years old, Winter, the ever adventurous and mischievous cat, remains a beloved member of our family. Her love for exploration and hunting hasn't diminished, but she always manages to make time to sit with my daughter and keep her company. And although she still considers me her secondary carer, I cherish the moments when she comes over and rests her head on my legs as she lounges on the sofa. But as much as I adore her, Winter still likes to play her little games, and on rainy days, she'll saunter across me with her wet paws, as if to remind me who's boss. But I wouldn't have it any other way. With her stunning looks and confident attitude, Winter knows how gorgeous she is, and I can only hope that someday she will love me as much as I love her.

13

CAT RESCUE

Max & Poppy

In this chapter, you'll discover how I found myself in the right place at the right time to come to the aid of my favourite animal... and not once, but twice.

Let me tell you about the first time. It was a beautiful summer's morning, and I was driving home from my night shift at a food warehouse. Suddenly, I witnessed the car in front of me hit a cat. I watched in horror as it was flung through the air before hitting the ground and landing on the roadside verge. The driver didn't stop to check on the poor puss and, of course, I couldn't just leave it there. I slammed on my brakes and pulled over. I could see the cat was hurt, and although it was hissing at me, I couldn't let it suffer; I had to do something.

I approached the cat slowly, trying to calm it down and gain its trust. It was angry and scared, and every time I tried to touch it, it would hiss and swat at me. I knew I had to be patient and gentle. I sat down beside it and started talking softly, saying I was there to help and that I meant no harm. After a while, the cat started to calm down, and I was able to stroke its head without it hissing or swatting. I knew I had to act quickly before its condition worsened, so I decided to try and pick it up and take it to the vet. But there was a small wire fence between us, and I didn't want to hurt the cat further by pulling it through the small holes. So,

I leaned over the fence and gently and swiftly lifted the cat by the scruff of its neck. To my relief, it didn't resist, and I was able to cradle it in my arms. I placed it in the passenger seat of my car and covered it with a blanket to keep it warm. I knew the RVC's Queen Mother Hospital for Animals in Hertfordshire was open 24/7 because they'd treated Ginge. So, I drove there as quickly as I could. When I arrived, I explained to the vet what had happened and left the cat in their care. I filled out a form with my details and said that if the injured puss didn't have an owner, I would happily take it in.

A week later, I received a phone call from a woman who asked if I was the person who had saved her pet. She was grateful for what I had done and told me that her cat's name was Max. She explained that Max had fully recovered from his injuries, and she was keeping him inside for the time being. She wanted to send me a thank you card to show her appreciation, and I gave her my address.

A few days later, I received a lovely letter from her.

Dear Amelia,

Just a small gift to say a big thank you for rescuing my cat, Max. You are a very kind lady, and I can't put into words the things I really want to say to you. Max is a rescue cat. I've had him three years now and really love him. We also have a female cat called Ellie who is fourteen years old; she is also a rescue. You are most welcome to come and see Max if you ever feel like it. Thank you once again for getting him the help he needed. He is feeling and looking a lot better today, and he is also sleeping a lot. Thanks again.

Enclosed was £50 worth of John Lewis vouchers. My daughter had recently turned one and taken her first steps, prompting friends and family to suggest that she needed a pair of 'cruising shoes', which are soft footwear designed for new walkers before they transition to proper shoes. I decided to use the vouchers to purchase a pair of these shoes, which I have kept as a cherished reminder of that special day.

Years later, after starting my own cat sitting business, I came across the letter Max's owner had sent to me. I decided to call her and offer my services. To my dismay, she told me that Max had been hit by a car again, and this time hadn't made it. She explained that she had let him out because he loved being outside, but she regretted it deeply and missed him dearly.

I felt terrible for the lady, and for Max. It was a heartbreaking end to a story that had started with me being in the right place at the right time. But I knew that I had done everything I could to help Max, and that gave me some comfort. I also knew that I would continue to help other cats in need and make a difference in their lives, just as I had done for Max.

R.I.P MAX X

***

On another ordinary morning, while taking my daughter to preschool, I stumbled upon a 'lost cat' poster nailed to our village noticeboard. It tugged on my heartstrings, as I knew how the owner would be consumed by worry and fear. Days later, I took my daughter to the park near our home and a cat wandered into view. There it stood, eyeing us curiously, as if it was contemplating whether to come over and say hello. I crouched down and beckoned it over, hoping to give it a little love and affection. But alas, it scampered away at the last moment. The cat returned a little while later, and that's when it hit me. Could this be the cat from the poster? I couldn't recall, so I whipped out my phone and snapped a quick photo of it, determined to investigate further. I called my daughter over and announced that we were going on an adventure. We rushed back to the poster and, lo and behold, the cat in my photo was a match. Without hesitation, I phoned the owner, Cherry, and told her where I had seen the cat. She was ecstatic to hear that we might have found her missing puss, who was called Poppy. We arranged to meet in the park, and while waiting, I called out for Poppy, but she failed to appear again. When Cherry arrived, I showed her the photo and tears filled her eyes. She explained that Poppy had gone missing after her mother had passed away, and it was a tough time for everyone.

We stood around chatting and calling for Poppy while Cherry left some treats for her in the nearby alleyway. Although she didn't appear, Cherry left the park feeling hopeful, and I promised to keep an eye out for her missing cat.

Over the next few days, I found myself returning to the park to search for Poppy. When she was still nowhere to be seen, I began to feel disheartened. I couldn't help but wonder if I had missed my chance to help this poor feline. But then, on the fourth day, something unexpected happened.

As my daughter had never been on a bus before, I decided to take her on one for a little trip into town. We went shopping and had lunch before hopping back on the bus. It was as we were walking past the park on our way home that I saw Poppy again. I quickly put down my bags and approached her, softly calling her name. To my surprise, she came over for a stroke and started purring. Feeling elated, I called Dave and asked him to bring a cat carrier to the park so we could take Poppy home – I didn't want to risk losing her again. Dave arrived a few minutes' later, but when we tried to pop Poppy in the carrier, she went ballistic. She scratched both my husband and me and tried to clamber over my shoulder. In the end, I had to resort to holding her by the scruff of her neck and gently pushing her into the carrier.

Once we got Poppy home, we gave her some food and water and let her calm down after her ordeal. Then Cherry arrived to collect her. It was an incredible feeling knowing that I had helped to reunite them.

A week after Poppy's return, Cherry invited me over to her cosy cottage for a cuppa. Cherry was clearly elated to have Poppy back, and she couldn't stop praising how quickly she had settled back in at home. I noticed that Cherry had another feline family member – a pure black, friendly cat named Fin, who immediately rubbed against my leg, begging for a stroke. As I obliged, Cherry began to tell me about Fin's incredible story of survival and resilience.

When Fin was just a kitten, he was diagnosed with lymphoma, a type of feline leukaemia that most cats don't survive. Cherry explained to me that she was lucky to have him with her after all these years, as happy and as healthy as ever. I couldn't help but be captivated by this little fighter's story. It was a testament to his bravery and spirit that he had survived such a deadly disease at such a young age.

Cherry went on to tell me about Fin's arrival into the family, which was nothing short of a chaotic, yet heart-warming, affair. The little one was a Christmas surprise for Cherry's 12-year-old daughter, and they vowed to keep him a secret till the big day. However, things didn't quite go according to plan. Cherry's daughter's half-sisters had also planned to visit and had decided between them to pick up the kitten on their way, leading to a logistical nightmare of managing luggage, presents, and a small carrier holding a three-month-old kitten. The two girls had to endure the hustle and bustle of packed trains and Tubes at the peak of Christmas time, all the while ensuring the safety of the fragile feline. At one point, they even found themselves laughing hysterically at the bottom of an escalator, surrounded by their scattered belongings. Meanwhile, Cherry was frantically trying to find a hiding spot for the kitten, where she could be kept until Christmas morning. She even approached her neighbour, but unfortunately, the neighbour was allergic to cats, leaving Cherry with no other option but to present the kitten to her daughter on Christmas Eve.

Despite the change in plans, Cherry's daughter instantly fell in love with the kitten, and the family's new addition became an irreplaceable part of their lives. The daughter chose his name, which was initially misheard by Cherry's mother, who thought they had named the kitten 'Sin'. It was a hilarious mix up that brought a smile to everyone's face.

As I sipped my tea and listened to Cherry's story, I couldn't help but appreciate the love and effort that went into making that Christmas so special. It was a beautiful reminder that the most meaningful and memorable stories often arise from the most unexpected and challenging circumstances.

Cherry went on to recount in detail Fin's incredible survival story. It all began when Cherry and her family went away for a weekend, leaving Fin with relatives. Upon their return, they found that Fin was lethargic and unwell. They took him to the vet and the diagnosis of lymphoma soon followed. The prognosis was not good. The vet warned that the chances of survival were slim, but Cherry was determined to try everything in her power to save her daughter's beloved companion. She agreed to a new treatment regimen consisting of chemotherapy and steroids, which was both risky and expensive. But she was willing to do whatever it took to give Fin a fighting chance. The results were miraculous. Fin not only survived the treatment, but he also thrived. He was one of the very few cats who have ever recovered from this type of cancer treatment, and his family was overjoyed.

After hearing this beautiful story, I felt grateful to have met Cherry, Poppy and Fin. I realised that sometimes, the best things in life come from unexpected encounters. Cherry and I went on to become good friends, and when I became a cat sitter, she asked me to look after Poppy and Fin on many occasions, which I was honoured to do. Poppy wasn't a fan of me at first, but we eventually became friends. Meanwhile, Fin and I became instant pals, and he would often lay on my feet while I stroked him. We would spread out on the floor together, heads touching and him purring his little heart out. He was always so happy and laid-back, and I loved him very much.

Sadly, in June 2022, I received a message from Cherry to say that Fin had passed away at the age of just nine. He had developed aggressive intestinal cancer, and this time no treatment was available. I was devastated for Cherry and her family, especially as Fin had fought so hard to stay in this world. However, I know that throughout his time on earth, he was adored by his family, and we will all remember him with love in our hearts.

R.I.P FIN XX

14

KATINKA & DAISY

Through a close friend, I heard about a man who was seeking a new home for his house cat. He was moving to a place where pets weren't allowed, and he desperately wanted to find a loving environment for his precious moggy. At that time, I wasn't entertaining the thought of adding another cat to our household. We already had our three cherished girls: Sushi, seventeen, Koshka, fourteen, and Winter, five.

But I'm not known as a crazy cat lady for nothing. Tentatively, I emailed the man for more details. He responded, "She's in perfect health and is delightfully contented. She's three years old and happens to be female. I'll send you some photos later."

I knew in that moment I was doomed. Once I'd seen her photo, I knew I was going to love her regardless.

It was a couple of days before I received an email containing a single image. It was all it took to capture my heart completely. This girl was breathtakingly beautiful, with an off-white coat flecked with grey, a grey face and ears, ringed grey legs and an elegantly patterned grey tail. Her eyes were soft blue, and although not as piercing as Winter's, they brimmed with their own unique beauty. But, as the old saying goes, looks aren't everything. Eager to know more about her temperament, I asked the man to describe it further. He replied, "She possesses a gentle nature, adores people, and gets along famously with other cats."

I had to admit that she sounded like the perfect addition to our family. However, one detail in particular really tugged at my heartstrings. This cat had never experienced the great outdoors, and at the age of three, had already given birth to two litters of kittens. With this in mind, I realised it was my calling to offer her a caring and nurturing home. Without hesitation, I emailed the man with my decision, and he offered to bring her to my house.

Now, given this cat's sheltered history, I felt a deep responsibility to give her the best life possible. I envisioned her revelling in the sensation of the wind rustling through her luxurious fur and the warm caress of the sun on her face. Of course, I planned to have her spayed once she had settled comfortably into her new surroundings. As I looked at her picture once more, admiring her beautiful fur, it dawned on me that she might possess a distinguished lineage. Intrigued, I reached out to the man again, curious to learn more about her breed. In response, he revealed that she is a British Shorthair, which explained her beautiful blue-grey colouring. Although I had never experienced the pleasure of sharing my life with a British Shorthair before, I knew their reputation for having affectionate natures.

Incredibly, British Shorthairs date back to the first century AD, when they are thought to have been brought to the UK by the Romans, who relied on them to keep their camps free from rodents. By the 19th century, these moggies had morphed into tough street cats, and this is when a visionary cat breeder named Harrison William Weir, fondly known as 'the father of the cat fancy,' embarked on a breeding programme with them. He even organised England's first-ever cat show, which was held in Crystal Palace, London, in 1871.

As time progressed, the British Shorthair we adore today received a touch of refinement. After World War I, breeders introduced Persian, Russian Blue, French Chartreux and Domestic Shorthair cats into the mix, perfecting the breed we know and love. By the 1970s, the British Shorthair had gained worldwide recognition and adoration. Today, there are approximately 30 variations of the British Shorthair.

What sets British Shorthairs apart is their easy-going, loyal and affectionate personalities. They effortlessly form deep bonds with their owners and have calm and collected natures. If they feel the slightest bit uneasy, they simply relocate to a more comfortable spot. While they may not be the biggest fans of being lifted into the air, they'll gladly cosy up beside you.

It's no wonder then that they are stars of literature and TV. They are reputed to have inspired the iconic Cheshire Cat from Lewis Carroll's *Alice in Wonderland*. Additionally, Puss in Boots, with his plump cheeks and enchanting eyes, is often regarded as a British Shorthair, despite his Spanish accent. And let's not forget about Arlene, Garfield's girlfriend in the movie adaptation of the famous comic strip, who is based on a British Blue.

Between 2011 and 2014, a tortoiseshell British Shorthair named Smokey held the record for the loudest purr, reaching an astonishing 67.7 decibels. That's some serious volume in the purr department. To top it all off, in 2022, the British Shorthair was among the eight felines featured on a series of postage stamps issued by the Royal Mail.

It was Christmastime 2022 when our new kitty joined the fold. As I gazed at her, a memory resurfaced from a beloved book I once read to my daughter called *Katinka's Tail*. The cat in the story was pure white, with a light and dark brown ringed tail, and she bore a striking resemblance to our little one. And so, Katinka had found her name.

For the first week, Katinka resided in our bedroom while we all got acquainted with each other. From the outset, she readily approached Dave and me for strokes, affectionately rubbing her face against our hands. Only unfamiliar sounds momentarily unsettled her, causing her to flatten her stomach against the floor or retreat to her bed until she was sure she was safe. But after two weeks, her fears had all but subsided. Now it was time to introduce her to her feline housemates, and we hoped the transition would be harmonious. We needn't have worried. With an air of familiarity, Katinka sauntered into the living room as if she had always lived with us. At first, my cats were hesitant, giving the occasional hiss and maintaining a safe distance, but gradually they began exchanging brief sniffs as they passed each other, testing the waters of friendship.

Katinka effortlessly charms us, albeit on her own terms. Although she prefers to sit beside us rather than on our laps and detests being lifted into the air, as is typical of her breed, her loyalty shines through. She is not particularly vocal but wants to be wherever we are, trailing contentedly from room to room after us.

After six months, she's gone from a cooped-up house cat to an intrepid outdoor explorer, revelling in the simple pleasures of nature. With the sun on her face and the wind in her fur, she frolics in the garden, chasing flies with an unwavering determination. Time seems to stand still as she loses herself in this thrilling feline pursuit. She's content to stay close to home, not venturing too far from the sanctuary of our garden. She hasn't quite got the hang of coming in and out through the cat flap yet, so for now we have resorted to taping it open, but nevertheless, I'm amazed at the progress she has made in such a short time. We relish the moments when she allows herself to be stroked, emitting a gentle purr that speaks volumes about her inner contentment. Although we're all still getting to know her, I'd say she is a calm soul who relishes her own company without needing to draw attention to herself. Whatever her true nature may be, one thing is certain – we adore her unconditionally. Our love for her knows no bounds and will endure for a lifetime.

Adding Katinka to our family has been an incredible blessing, and she has woven herself into the tapestry of our hearts.

**

I didn't intend on having anymore cats, but July 2023 had other plans for me. Just a few days after we lost Koshka, I received a message from someone who urgently needed to rehome her pet cat, who she had owned since she was a kitten. Sadly, her new baby was allergic to her, so the woman had no choice but to let her go.

I felt torn. I was still grieving Koshka, and replacing her with another cat so soon didn't feel right somehow. On the other hand, I knew I could give this animal in need a loving home. Her owner sent me her photograph, and I saw a cat with incredible poise who already seemed destined to join our clan.

When she arrived, her spirited nature was unmistakable, and it didn't take us long to christen her (Crazy) Daisy. We arranged to have her spayed and, as she settled down, a new facet of her personality emerged that revealed her as a loyal and steadfast companion. She would follow me around the house so much it was like having a second shadow.

I did some research online and discovered that Daisy is a tortie point Siamese – a breed known for its vocal prowess and distinctive tortoiseshell coat. This made sense, as Daisy certainly doesn't hold back when it comes to expressing her opinions.

What brought me the most joy, however, was how well Daisy bonded with Katinka. Their camaraderie was instant, like two kindred spirits recognising each other across a crowded room. Seeing them together, I know I made the right decision in welcoming Daisy into our home.

DAISY

KATINKA

15
DREAMIES

My feline companions have always possessed an insatiable hunger for Dreamies – those irresistible treats that make their tails twitch with delight. One day, while unpacking my supermarket haul, I noticed a promotional code on the Dreamies packet that promised a chance to win something exciting. Though I don't usually bother with such competitions, the prospect of landing something cat-related piqued my interest, and I decided to give it a shot.

Little did I know that this impulsive decision would set off a chain of events that would change my life for the better. Picture a scorching summer day, where the heat is unbearable, and a gentle breeze but a distant memory. It was on a day like this that my clumsiness led to the demise of a once pristine glass table, now shattered beyond repair. Desperate for a replacement, I found myself succumbing to a spur-of-the-moment purchase; a magnificent rattan garden sofa set that had an air of elegance and comfort. Regrettably, I had failed to consult my dear husband before making this audacious acquisition, and thus the stage was set for a spirited debate over my spending habits. But even his grumbling couldn't dampen my enthusiasm for the furniture, especially when my feline friends took an immediate liking to the luxurious sofa.

And then, just when I thought my luck couldn't get any better, an email appeared in my inbox – I had won the Dreamies prize draw and a whopping £1,000! Though initially sceptical, a phone call with a Dreamies representative quickly dispelled my doubts, and I was overjoyed to learn that I had most certainly won the grand prize. Not only did this unexpected windfall make me feel like a champ, but it also meant that my garden furniture was effectively free.

As I twirled and danced around my kitchen, a pack of Dreamies in hand, I couldn't help but feel that this stroke of good fortune was meant to be.

So, to anyone out there who chances upon a promotional code, heed my advice and take the plunge because you never know what amazing opportunities might be waiting for you. And if you are a devoted cat lover like me, then rest assured, anything feline-related is worth a shot.

16
CAT FESTIVALS/SHOWS

On the memorable day of July 29th, 2019, something magical awaited me on the outskirts of the capital – a cat festival unlike anything I had ever experienced. From the moment I read about it online, my imagination was ignited. A world entirely devoted to feline wonders beckoned me, and I knew I had to be there. Naturally, I invited a couple of my fellow cat aficionados, plus Dave and my daughter, who was then five. To my delight, they eagerly accepted the invitation. So, off we ventured to the town of Beckenham, the sun casting its warm glow upon us, heightening my anticipation for the day ahead.

When we arrived, we received vibrant green wristbands in exchange for our tickets and were instantly immersed in the colourful ambience of the festival. Dave and my daughter scurried off to the face painting tent while my friends and I entered the expansive marquee to be met with a sea of people who shared my love for all things feline. The stalls before us showcased an (p)awe-inspiring array of merchandise, catering to every imaginable desire or need a cat may have. From captivating toys and mesmerising water fountains to soft, cosy blankets, luxurious beds and towering scratching posts, the options seemed endless. I couldn't help but marvel at the abundance of cat-related wonders laid out before me. It was a true paradise for ailurophiles.

Amidst the crowd, a lady gracefully wandered about with an astonishingly lifelike animatronic cat perched on her shoulder. The intricate details were mesmerising – the cat's head swayed, its tail gracefully flicked, and its eyes blinked with an uncanny realism. I had never encountered such a convincing creation, and I found myself in sheer awe of its artistry. As I continued my journey through the marquee, a stunning Sphynx cat, serenely perched atop a majestic cat tower, caught my eye. I approached the creature and kindly asked its owner if I could stroke her. With a nod of approval, I delicately caressed the Sphynx's velvety skin and, before I knew it, a crowd had gathered, eager to partake in this serene encounter. The Sphynx remained unfazed, giving out an air of tranquillity and star-like poise, as if she were accustomed to such adoration. Leaving her to her newfound admirers, I resumed my exploration, indulging myself in some delightful purchases, including six pairs of socks decorated with a cat resembling my beloved feline companion, Shakira, a cat toy and some treats for the beauties that waited for me at home. Along my journey, kind souls offered me free pin badges, and I accepted one that proudly proclaimed me a 'Crazy Cat Lady' – a title that I accepted with utmost pride.

When I was finally reunited with Dave and my daughter, I saw that her face had been transformed into an enchanting fusion of a cat and a unicorn. "I'm a caticorn," my daughter proudly informed me.

Our eyes were then drawn to a lady sipping a refreshing drink out of a coconut, and without hesitation, we bought one for my daughter, seeing her face light up with happiness as she savoured the tropical treat. Seeking respite from the heat, we settled under the shade of a majestic tree to rest for a while.

Eventually, my adventurous spirit compelled me to explore a different corner of the festival. Two queues beckoned for attention – one leading to an exquisite display of cat art, and the other to a room housing cats and kittens in need of loving homes. Alas, Dave had firmly warned me to steer clear of the latter, forbidding any possibility of expanding our feline family. Reluctantly, I joined the art queue, where I struck up lively conversations with fellow cat enthusiasts. Their heartfelt tales of adoration for their furry companions resonated deeply with me. Some proudly shared stories of their ten beloved cats, and I couldn't help but feel a sense of kinship. I confided that I had seven feline friends, but that the number had once also been in double digits. Surprisingly, instead of being seen as peculiar or excessive, I was embraced as a member of a special club. It was a moment of sheer connection, and I felt as if I had finally found my tribe.

As I patiently waited in line, a man emerged with an extraordinary cat perched on his shoulder. The calico was more than happy to accept the affectionate caresses of passers-by as the man explained it was an emotional support pet and had played an instrumental role in brightening his days and helping him overcome life's challenges. As the duo glided by me, I couldn't resist giving the cat a gentle tickle under its chin.

Finally, my turn arrived, and I stepped into the art room, where a plethora of cat-inspired creations surrounded me. My eyes wandered from one mesmerising piece to another, and I was completely engrossed in their beauty. My gaze was then drawn to a magnificent grey cat bedecked in jewels and nestled within a lotus flower. It was accompanied by a whimsical gathering of other feline creatures – a cat bumble bee and a cat lady bird. This exquisite artwork was unlike anything I had ever seen before, and just above it on the wall hung another masterpiece by the same artist, Lynda Bell. It depicted a girl with auburn hair encircled by a symphony of fifteen cats. The picture seemed to pull me into its magical realm. And below it, yet another artwork grabbed my attention, a lone tabby cat donning a red wizard hat and a medallion, its emerald eyes exuding a commanding aura. The air seemed to crackle with a sense of mystique. I stood there for what felt like an eternity, torn between these extraordinary pieces, each carrying its own unique allure. Ultimately, the girl with the auburn hair resonated deeply with my own experiences of love and companionship, while the other painting reflected the joy and playfulness of a life shared with cats.

As my indecision prevailed, I reluctantly left the art room without purchasing any of the pieces. I then discovered Dave and my daughter and friends lounging beneath the very tree where I had left them earlier. I eagerly joined them, listening to the live music drifting through the air from a nearby stage and reflecting on a perfect day.

***

Following the festival, I couldn't wait for the next cat event to come along, and when I stumbled on an advertisement for LondonCats International Show, which was taking place on January 11th, 2020, in Central London, I booked tickets without hesitation. This time, there was an irresistible promise to meet a brand-new breed known as the Lykoi – the elusive, so-called 'werewolf cat'. The mere thought of getting up close and personal with a creature resembling a mystical werewolf sent chills down my spine. I couldn't resist the chance to find out more about its personality and perhaps even caress its otherworldly fur. To prepare myself for the momentous occasion, I delved into some online research, eager to uncover the origins and characteristics of this fascinating breed, which I relay in Chapter 18.

Finally, the big day arrived. I gazed in wonder at the cats on show, who were either lounging in their own giant cat carriers or out in the open, where they could fully bask in the adoration of the crowd. The first cat I met was a serene and laid-back Toyger, a breed resembling a miniature tiger, who blissfully snoozed while welcoming the gentle strokes of countless admirers. Unfazed by the attention, the Toyger exuded contentment. Next, I encountered a Sphynx, which I witnessed gracefully leap up to catch a cat toy being dangled by its doting owner. I was then graced with the presence of an American Curl, which had the fluffiness of a Maine Coon, a heavy mane, and distinctive ears that curled backwards. My final cat catchups were with a regal Scottish Fold, who are easy to identify because of their folded-down ears, an array of fluffy Persians, some beauteous Ragdolls, and a giant Maine Coon with an extraordinary fluffy mane and colossal paws.

Next came my much-anticipated meeting with the Lykoi. A crowd surrounded the booth where the werewolf cat, Bram, resided. Patiently awaiting my turn, I eventually found myself seated next to Bram's devoted owner. We exchanged greetings and introduced ourselves, and then I turned my attention to Bram, a creature of extraordinary beauty. The name werewolf cat suddenly made perfect sense, for his every feature bore an uncanny resemblance to that of a mythical werewolf. To my eyes, he was a living masterpiece. Overwhelmed by his presence, I timidly asked if I could stroke him and, to my delight, the owner graciously consented. Bram's fur appeared coarse and wiry, but I found myself caressing a soft and velvety coat. There was no trace of fear or timidity in his demeanour, and he exuded confidence. Seated regally, he embraced the attention and captivated me with his mesmerising yellow eyes. At one point, Bram extended his paw, which was a sight to behold. While other cats' toes are typically obscured by a sea of fur, Bram's were balding and resembled tiny monkey feet, each toe defined with precision. I couldn't thank Bram's owner enough for allowing me this unique encounter, which I'll never forget.

Following my time with Bram, an extraordinary turn of events unfolded, and Bram's gracious owner generously granted me an exclusive audience with him, which I also explore in Chapter 18.

***

In 2022, my insatiable curiosity led me to not one, but two further shows that left an indelible mark on my feline-loving soul. The first of these magnificent events was a Cat Extravaganza put on by the LCWW Group, which stands for Loving Cats Worldwide, in the town of Ware, Hertfordshire. My family and I couldn't wait to step once more into a realm where cats reigned supreme. Again, we were met with myriad felines, who were being paraded through the judging area. The Sphynxes, with their alluring, hairless bodies, appeared otherworldly, while the mischievous Devon Rexes flaunted their wavy curls with playful elegance. The Ragdolls, with their serene blue eyes, exuded tranquillity, and the British Shorthairs exhibited an irresistible aristocratic charm. Towering above them all, the magnificent Maine Coons emanated a grandeur befitting their majestic lineage. And, in the midst of it all, the Bengals, with their exotic markings, reminded us of the untamed spirit that lies within these domesticated animals.

The pride and joy of the cat owners was palpable, as they eagerly shared tales of cherished moments with these extraordinary animals. We learned of the journeys that brought the cats into their lives – the chance encounters, the serendipitous connections, and the unbreakable bonds formed over time. Each cage was adorned with an array of rosettes, proudly displayed as badges of honour for the achievements the cats had garnered in various competitions. The owners regaled us with stories of their triumphs, recounting the meticulous care and dedication they had poured into nurturing their remarkable feline superstars.

While the show cats revelled in their well-deserved recognition, our attention was also drawn to the delightful presence of some playful kittens, whose infectious energy filled the air. These tiny bundles of joy, with their unbound curiosity and endearing clumsiness, captured the hearts of all who crossed their path. They embodied the promise of future grace and beauty, a testament to the ongoing legacy of these esteemed breeds.

We watched on as the judges meticulously examined each cat, assessing their body structure and build and scrutinising the quality of their exquisite coats. They explained their decision-making process, shedding light on each breed's history, specific standards, and the traits they looked for. It was a truly enlightening experience, and it deepened our appreciation for the immense diversity and rich heritage of these feline wonders.

Beyond the spectacle of the judging arena, we delved into a marketplace of cat-themed treasures. My daughter was delighted when she stumbled upon a long, striped, green-feathered cat toy, which would be perfect for Winter as green is her favourite colour. Who would have thought that cats have colour preferences? Well, I can tell you they do. For myself, I bought some intricately designed cat coasters and two exquisite cat necklaces.

Overall, this cat show not only celebrated the beauty and grace of our feline friends but also fostered a sense of community among cat enthusiasts. It was a day filled with joy, discovery and an overwhelming appreciation for the bond between humans and cats.

The following weekend, we headed to The Supreme Show, which is run by the Governing Council of the Cat Fancy (the GCCF), an organisation renowned for hosting grand events in the feline world. This time, the show took place in Kenilworth, a picturesque market town in Warwickshire, about an hour and a half's drive from our home in Hertfordshire.

When we arrived, we were handed wristbands, and I was awestruck by the sheer magnitude of the show. It was unlike anything I had ever seen before, with a massive turnout of enthusiastic cat lovers. Everywhere I looked, there were numbered pens adorned with elaborate decorations. The show's theme was the Queen's Jubilee, and the level of creativity and attention to detail in the pens' designs was outstanding. One stood out, in particular, as it had a horse and cart stationed in front of it and was flanked by life-size cardboard cut-outs of the Queen's guards. Above the enclosure were small replicas of the Millennium Wheel, Big Ben and other iconic London landmarks. Each pen seemed to outdo the next in terms of artistic flair and imagination. I was equally impressed with the blue velvet pen, complete with luxurious cushions and a regally reclining cat. Another pen featured a cat dressed in a Union Jack dress. Some of the other pens boasted opulent gold curtains, drapes and satin cushions. But to my mind, the creativity peaked in a pen that was home to a grey cat. Beside him hung his portrait, and he dressed as a king with a crown, a giant gold collar and royal robes. It was a remarkable and amusing sight, showcasing the passion, dedication and eccentricity of the owners.

The variety of cat breeds on display seemed endless, and we made a point of exploring every corner of the venue. The judging area drew us in once again, to where the cats basked in the gaze of the onlookers. Rosettes adorned most of the cat pens, allowing us glimpses into the impressive achievements of these feline beauties. Some proclaimed 'First', others displayed 'Best of Breed', and one even boasted the coveted title of 'Overall Best in Show'.

During our recce, we encountered an Egyptian Mau, a breed I had only read about before. They are usually grey and have predominant spots and stripes, making them beautiful to look at. I relished the opportunity to stroke one in person. Lastly, two exotic shorthairs won us over with their irrepressible charm.

After indulging ourselves in the world of cats, we ventured into the adjoining hall, where an awe-inspiring array of cat-related merchandise awaited us. The sight was overwhelming – an entire marketplace dedicated to feline treasures. We couldn't resist picking up a few items from the Cats Protection stall, including a delightful stationary set.

The GCCF Supreme Cat Show was an extraordinary event, although the atmosphere was noticeably more focused and intense compared to the previous shows we'd attended. Understandably, the owners were nervously awaiting the moment their cats would be called for judging, leaving little room for casual conversation. While I would have loved the opportunity to delve deeper into the fascinating world of cat shows and hear the stories behind each feline participant, I appreciated the dedication and seriousness of the event.

Nevertheless, the showcase of cats from various breeds was a sight to behold. Their impeccable grooming, poise and distinctive personalities were a testament to the passion and commitment of their owners. It was a privilege to witness such incredible feline beauty and diversity. I was left with a renewed appreciation for the dedication and love that goes into showcasing these remarkable animals.

To each cat that graced these events, I applaud you for your exceptional presence and thank you for making the occasions truly extraordinary.

17
LYNDA BELL

In July 2019, at the cat festival in the previous chapter, I fell in love with the work of the artist Lynda Bell. Here is one of her creations that I saw at the show.

Following the festival, I followed Lynda on social media as I wanted to see more of her creations; viewing them felt like being transported to a wonderland. Then I noticed that Lynda was holding a raffle, and the prize was her artwork. I bought some tickets and was over the moon to win an original painting of hers called the 'Snow Maid', which now hangs in my daughter's bedroom. I also won a fine art print, which I have displayed in my office. Winning the pieces felt like destiny – I had only been introduced to Lynda's work a month earlier and now I was the proud owner of two of her pieces.

Here is some information about Lynda.

Lynda is a full-time painter and illustrator living in New Zealand. She is trained in fine arts, painting, teaching and arts therapy and brings all of this learning into her art practice. She strives to embed happiness and inspiration into each artwork and believes that joy and kindness can change the world. Her artwork is largely motivated by her love of animals and her desire to awaken kindness and compassion within her viewers.

Within her paintings, stories unfold, and the viewers are taken into a world where animals are treated with respect and kindness; a world where anything is possible, and stories are abundant. It is within this world that people may be reminded of the integral part of their self which forms their humanity: compassion, love and a kinship with animals that we all felt as young children.

You can find Lynda at www.artbylyndabell.com or follow her on Facebook by searching for Lynda Bell Art.

Lynda currently owns two cats, Billy and Lily. This is the painting that captured my heart; it has to be my all-time favourite.

18
THE LYKOI

Pronounced lie koi, meaning werewolf cat

Months after attending the cat show where I first encountered Nicola, the owner of the Lykoi cat named Bram, we set a date for me to travel to Nicola's home, a two hour-drive from my own, and discover more about the breed, which came into existence through a remarkable natural mutation, only discovered in the US in 2010. The mother of one of the litters where the mutation was discovered was a black domestic shorthair. Initially, it was thought to be a spontaneous Sphynx mutation. However, DNA testing revealed that the kittens lacked the Sphynx cat gene. Further investigations were conducted to rule out any diseases or disorders that might account for the cats' distinct hair and coats. Remarkably, no medical explanations were found to explain their unique coat pattern and the animals were found to be in overall good health. It was conclusively determined that Lykoi cats were indeed a genuine natural mutation.

The name 'Lykoi' originates from the Greek word 'lykos', meaning wolf. This breed is often referred to as the 'werewolf cat' due to its unusual appearance. The skin around the cats' eyes, nose, muzzle and chin is hairless, creating a mask-like appearance. Similarly, their legs and paws are also devoid of hair, contributing to the popular werewolf resemblance. An intriguing aspect of the Lykoi is their so-called roan coat, a pattern of intermixed white and coloured guard hairs. While this pattern can be found in other animals, such as horses, it hasn't been observed in any other cat breed. Additionally, Lykoi cats lack an undercoat, which makes them more susceptible to extreme temperatures. Renowned for their dog-like behaviour, Lykoi cats are friendly, affectionate, extroverted and active. At times, they can shed some or all of their coat, making them look rather naked. This is perfectly normal, and the coats do grow back.

During my brief meeting with Nicola at the cat show in 2019, she mentioned that in addition to Bram, who she introduced me to, she had another extraordinary Lykoi named Major Tom. Not only that, but Nicola also had a few more feline friends and other animals she was keen for me to meet.

As I drove into Nicola's road, my excitement peaked when I noticed darker-coloured roof tiles forming the word cat in capitals and a concrete cat perched on top of the roof, seemingly keeping watch. It was a clear sign that I had indeed found the right place. I also noticed how Nicola had a cat-themed number plate like my own. What a coincidence!

Nicola greeted me warmly at the door and explained that her house was aptly named Hieronymus House in honour of her beloved Devon Rex, who had sadly now passed away. Hieronymus, affectionately nicknamed Little H, was named after the 15th century artist Hieronymus Bosch. The name itself means 'sacred one'. We then settled down with a cup of tea, and Nicola began sharing heart-warming stories about Hieronymus.

Little H was not just a pet, he was Nicola's best friend. Born with missing joints in three legs and an improperly formed hip socket, he faced significant challenges from the start. Initially tiny and underweight, Nicola took it upon herself to bottle feed him, and she kept him in her bed to provide warmth and comfort.

Every day, she weighed him, uncertain if he would survive. But with gradual weight gain and remarkable progress, he transformed into an amazing boy who captured Nicola's heart completely. From then on, their bond was unbreakable. Whenever she went out, Hieronymus would eagerly wait for Nicola's return, descending the stairs as best he could to greet her. He would also sit at her feet, patiently waiting to be picked up, like a toddler yearning for cuddles. Sadly, at the age of eight, he suddenly and tragically passed away due to kidney failure. Nicola's eyes welled up with tears as she shared his story, the pain of losing him still raw. In his short life, Hieronymus touched the hearts of everyone who knew him and proved to be a true survivor. Despite his disability, he was a social butterfly, winning over everyone who crossed his path. Nicola used to throw birthday parties for him, drawing guests from far and wide who brought cards and gifts for her special boy. Since her cat, Beleela, also has disabilities, Nicola decided to celebrate her birthday every year on what would have been Hieronymus's big day. Nicola emphasised the importance of treasuring the cats we have, and recognising the blessings they bring into our lives. Hieronymus sounded like a one-in-a-million feline companion, and I wish I could have met him in person.

As Nicola continued sharing details about her furry family, she mentioned that all her moggies were indoor cats and had been neutered, except for Bram, the Lykoi, who was scheduled for neutering soon. A proud fan of David Bowie, Nicola playfully hinted at references to the music legend in relation to her cats. So, any David Bowie enthusiasts should try and spot those delightful connections. At one point, Nicola even had a cat called David, though he is no longer with her. She explained how her deep love of animals had led her to being vegan from a young age.

As I delved further into Nicola's feline world, I was introduced

to Beleela, whom she had adopted in memory of Hieronymus. She had a white chest and a black head, ears and tail, and Nicola rescued her from a charitable organisation that had brought her all the way from Egypt, where she had been surviving as a street cat. Interestingly, Beleela's name derives from an Egyptian porridge, adding a touch of cultural flavour to her story. Her hind legs were injured in a car accident when she was young, rendering them immobile. However, this resilient feline was able to drag herself around, undeterred by her physical limitations. She had mastered the use of litter trays and even tackled stairs like any able-bodied cat. Beleela possessed a remarkable spirit and, on a few occasions, she scooted past me, allowing me the privilege of stroking her silky fur. It was evident that she was living life to the fullest and relishing every moment.

Nicola also shared exciting news about another disabled cat soon to join their household. Blinchik, a tabby and white cat from Cyprus, was discovered abandoned in a field and struggling to walk due to nerve damage. His name translated as 'Russian pancake', and given his and Beleela's breakfast-themed names, it seemed destined that they would forge a special bond. Nicola informed me that Blinchik was set to arrive in the coming month, and I eagerly anticipated meeting this resilient newcomer.

Nicola went on to reminisce about two beloved cats who had passed away earlier that year. Dorothy, a dramatic Devon Rex, whose pedigree name was Yassassin Killer Queen, succumbed to a stroke at the age of 13. Oberon, an endearing Sphynx known for his charismatic personality, peacefully departed this earth at the age of 12, after being diagnosed with a heart murmur and, later, colitis. Nicola showed me treasured photographs of Dorothy and Oberon, and I could sense the lingering feeling of loss she had for these cherished kitties.

My feline journey continued when I had the pleasure of meeting some more of Nicola's cats. Pandora, Jinx and Lucien formed an impressive trio. Pandora, a stunning silver tabby, approached me with unreserved affection. Her purr resonated like a finely tuned motor, and it was impossible not to instantly fall in love with her. Her pedigree name, Lady Stardust, added a touch of mystique to her presence. Lily, a Devon Rex, happened to be Pandora's offspring. Jinx, a black smoke cat, is half Burmese and half Devon Rex, and he displayed a more reserved demeanour. His pedigree name is Mr Jinx, and he cautiously sniffed me before gradually warming up, particularly after I offered him a few tempting cat treats. Lucien, who is affectionately known as Baba, was the distinguished elder statesman of the family, approaching an impressive age of 15. In his younger days, Lucien had earned second place in the GCCF's Supreme Cat Show, and when I first encountered him, he was cosily wrapped up in a blanket, as comfy as a cat can be. Upon hearing my greeting, he emerged with a contented purr that embodied both wisdom and gentleness. Lucien gracefully accepted strokes, as if not wanting to miss out on any attention. Eventually, he returned to his warm blanket, still purring, keeping watch over us. In April 2024, since writing this, Lucien unfortunately passed away at the grand old age of 16. Nicola told me how all the cats had heat pads in their beds and loved their cosy spots. She then regaled me with tales of Esmerelda, the first Devon Rex she had ever owned, who had sadly passed away. Her current Esmerelda, shortened to Esme, had inherited her predecessor's name and was a black smoke Devon Rex. Esme preferred to remain upstairs and had a more independent and neurotic nature. She had specific dietary needs and could only eat chicken and a special type of biscuit. While Esme had a lovely temperament, Nicola explained how she sought attention on her own terms and wasn't particularly fond of other cats.

Eager to explore more of Nicola's feline haven, I followed her into another room, where I encountered three more of her extraordinary housemates: Lazarus, Lilly and Major Tom, a Lykoi with an air of mystery surrounding him. As I glanced at Lilly and Lazarus, I found it nearly impossible to tell them apart, as they were so similar. Lily, a black smoke Devon Rex, possessed an endearing and outgoing nature akin to her mother, Pandora, whom I'd had the pleasure of meeting earlier. The resemblance in their personalities was evident, as Lilly eagerly sought my affection and happily settled on my lap, indulging in endless cuddles. Her pedigree name is Yassassin Lilly Bug Stardust.

Lazarus, another black smoke, possessed a mischievous streak, which was revealed when he tried to nab a bit of the cake we were enjoying. He also had a unique way of expressing his fondness for others by affectionally nibbling them. This sweet and friendly boy had even earned the prestigious title of a cat show champion. His mother was none other than Esme.

However, the true highlight of my visit still awaited me, and I finally set my eyes on Major Tom, the stunning Lykoi. Nicola warned me that he was wary of strangers, and she advised me to approach him slowly, displaying disinterest to alleviate any sense of threat. With a handful of cat treats to pique his curiosity, I directed my attention towards him. He sat regally in his chair, reminding me of a star from the silver screen awaiting the dedicated attention of his entourage. In all my years, I have never encountered a cat like Major Tom, and every second in his presence felt like a remarkable privilege. His large, round, yellow eyes glowed with intensity, while the balding mask around his eyes only accentuated his hypnotic charm. Meanwhile, his elegantly elongated ears added to his wild and untamed presence. He was everything I had imagined, and more.

Approaching him cautiously, I offered Major Tom a treat, which he willingly accepted. As our connection deepened, I couldn't resist smiling and holding out another treat for him. He sniffed it, then delicately took it from my hand with his mouth – an act that filled my heart with sheer joy. It was then that his purring commenced, a melodic confirmation that I had earned his trust. Seizing the opportunity, I leaned in to stroke his fur, which was black with grey flecks and surprisingly soft and fine, like delicate kitten fur. This intimate moment felt like such an honour, as if I had been granted an audience with royalty. His strong and muscular body further attested to his power, and his long, wispy tail reminded me of a rat's. Sparse hair sporadically adorned its length, culminating in a completely bald end – a feature that added to its allure. As he curled up on his chair, I continued to stroke him and, in that moment, took my chance to glimpse at his monkey-like feet, which were wrinkled and predominant, yet undeniably beautiful. The absence of any fur only drew more attention to their unique appeal. Nicola's love for Major Tom was evident, and she eagerly shared details about him. At four years old, he is the son of the first Lykoi born in the UK, and he has a gentle nature with a trace of feral, which is evident when he is on high alert. Nicola revealed that her fascination with Lykois began at a cat show, where she fell in love with their unparalleled beauty.

My encounter with Major Tom shattered any preconceived notions I held about the Lykoi breed. Rather than a solitary and enigmatic creature, he proved to be the epitome of warmth and openness and remained unflinchingly present throughout my visit. Before bidding farewell to him, I couldn't resist expressing my gratitude with a gentle kiss on his head – a privilege I doubt I will experience again. Undoubtedly, Major Tom is a truly exquisite feline, and I shall forever remain grateful to Nicola for the opportunity to meet him.

After bidding farewell to Major Tom, I inquired about Bram. Nicola divulged that he tended to shy away from unfamiliar faces. At three years old, he shared Major Tom's striking black roan coat and boasted the pedigree name Bram Black Star. However, Nicola said there were distinct differences between the two Lykois, and she attributed Major Tom's sociability and laid-back nature to his unique breeding line. However, both of her Lykois possessed a certain feral quality that set them apart from Nicola's other cats. I inquired about any health issues specific to the Lykoi breed. Nicola told me that as a relatively new breed, any observed health concerns were minimal, with the only notable quirk being the occasional need to clean their greasy nails. Only time would reveal more about the breed's overall wellbeing.

Venturing further into Nicola's realm, I saw a black cat quickly dart away, seeking refuge from unfamiliar visitors. Nicola introduced her as Precious, a black moggy who exhibited a deep wariness towards strangers. Nicola shared the heart-breaking tale of Precious's previous litter of five kittens, who were fathered by Bram. Tragically, all of them succumbed to something known as Fading Kitten Syndrome. Nicola explained how they had inexplicably wasted away, one after the other, despite receiving veterinary care. Watching their young lives slip away was a profoundly sorrowful experience for Nicola.

We strolled into Nicola's garden, where a delightful surprise awaited me – a Muscovy duck that she had hatched herself, endearingly named Little Egg. Remarkably tame, Little Egg allowed me the rare privilege of cradling and cuddling a duck, which was an entirely new experience for me. Nicola also had two turkeys, Gloria and Hope, who had been rescued just in time before Christmas. She also introduced me to Riff Raff, a rescue hedgehog that was being cared for indoors until spring, when it would be released into the wild. As we continued our journey, we encountered some former factory chickens accompanied by a proud cockerel named Rodney. Finally, we met Nicola's diverse assortment of other ducks, including Mallards, Runner Ducks and six endearing little Call Ducks, no larger than pigeons, whom she fondly referred to as her 'Diddy Ducks'.

Returning indoors, Nicola shared with me the rosettes her cats had earned at various shows. Though she no longer frequented competitions, the memories forged and the pride she'd gained from receiving the awards will clearly stay with her forever.

With heartfelt gratitude, I extended my thanks to Nicola for inviting me to meet her one-of-a-kind family; a captivating array of felines and an enchanting menagerie of other beloved creatures. The encounter left an indelible imprint on my heart and reminded me of the deep love and cherished relationships between humans and their beloved furry, and feathered, friends.

19
CAT SITTING

Dave has always admired my unique connection with cats. He believes I truly understand them and possess extensive knowledge about their behaviours. In fact, he suggested that I start my own cat sitting business. Initially, I dismissed the idea, as I had no idea where to start when it came to setting one up. However, in 2017, I finished writing my memoir, *What Nobody Knew*, about my troubled early years. Penning it consumed a significant amount of my time, prompting me to leave my full-time job.

While working on the follow-up book, *Let Go of What You Know*, I found myself missing a more regular income, and Dave's idea of cat sitting resurfaced. After careful deliberation, I had to admit that my genuine love for cats and the prospect of being paid to spend time with them was undeniably appealing. Motivated by this revelation, I decided to delve deeper into the world of cat sitting.

My first step was to research the requirements for becoming a professional cat sitter. I wanted to adhere to the same high standards I would expect from someone caring for my own cats. I thoroughly studied the necessary information and felt confident in my ability to fulfil the role. To gauge the demand, I spoke to the 'cat people' in my area, who all said they would be interested in

such a service. Excited by this potential opportunity, I embarked on the necessary preparations.

First and foremost, I recognised the importance of establishing trust with my clients. So, I obtained a DBS check to prove that I didn't have a criminal record. Presenting the document during the initial client meeting assured my customers of my reliability and gave them peace of mind when it came to me entering their home. Furthermore, I acquired public liability insurance to protect both myself and the clients from any accidental damage that might occur. In addition to these essential elements, I wanted to create a visually appealing and memorable identity for my business. So, I collaborated with the designer who worked on the front cover of my first book, and we developed a simple business card featuring cat paws. I believed the design would attract the attention of potential customers more effectively than a standard business card.

To streamline my process, I designed a set of paperwork to bring along when meeting the client for the first time. I left space for the clients' and cats' names, plus the cats' dietary requirements, daily feeding routine, vital veterinarian details, medical history, indoor or outdoor preferences and litter tray information. Gathering as much relevant information as possible could only enhance the quality of care I provided.

With all these preparations in place, I strategically displayed posters in prominent locations, distributed business cards to potential clients, and even advertised my services on the back of my car.

That was back in 2018. Fast forward six years, and I can proudly say that my business has flourished, and I have garnered a healthy client base. The profession has become an integral part of my life, seamlessly blending into my identity as if it were always meant to be. I'm genuinely passionate about what I do, and I find immense joy in the company of cats and their diverse personalities. Each feline I encounter possesses their own unique traits, making every experience truly special.

Throughout my cat sitting career, I've been fortunate to encounter few challenges. However, the road has been dotted with unforgettable stories that have unfolded along the way. In this chapter, I'll share a few of these tales with you, granting you a window into the colourful world of cat sitting.

My first tale comes from my early days in business. During an initial meeting with a new client, I jotted down important details about her cat. As it was out of the house, I casually asked if she had a picture of her furry friend. To my surprise, she didn't have one to hand. Undeterred, she proceeded to describe her cat to me – a black and white furball, who was shy at first, until he had warmed to you.

The meeting went well, and I was booked for the job. When the day arrived, I was brimming with anticipation as I approached the house expecting to encounter a timid and skittish feline. Peering through the patio doors, I spotted a black and white cat leisurely lounging in the garden. Determined not to startle him, I devised a cunning plan. Before opening the door, I decided to make his breakfast. You see, I believe that food has the magical power to win over any cat's heart. So, with a cat food pouch in hand, I enthusiastically showed it to him through the glass, shouting, "Do you want your breakfast? Yum, you have salmon this morning!" My hope was that this display would assure him I was no threat, but the purveyor of delicious sustenance.

After transferring the food to a bowl, I placed it on the floor and triumphantly swung open the patio door, beckoning the cat to approach. To my delight, he happily trotted over and started rubbing against my legs. It seemed I had effortlessly won him over.

We bonded as if we were long-lost companions. I couldn't help but bask in my newfound title as the 'cat whisperer' who could tame even the most timid of felines.

But alas, my time of glory was short lived. After four days, the client checked in with me, curious about our progress. Brimming with confidence, I relayed the monumental achievement of our blossoming relationship. The client responded, "That's fantastic! Can you send me a picture of you both? I'd love to see it." Filled with pride, I eagerly snapped a cat selfie and promptly shared it with her. Her reply arrived seconds later. It read, "Thank you for the photo, but that's not my cat. The real one usually hides under the bed. This imposter sneaks in, and I have no idea who he belongs to."

Oh, the shame I felt!

I turned to the invader cat, who seemed to smirk in amusement, as if he had pulled off the greatest cat caper of all time. With a gentle nudge out the back door, I bid him farewell and swiftly searched under the bed. Lo and behold, there was the genuine article – a cat strikingly similar to the imposter but with subtle facial markings that set them apart. Filled with remorse, I offered the real cat his meal, apologising profusely for my blunder. Although I tried to make amends during the remaining time I had with him, I couldn't shake the feeling that he was fully aware and disapproving of my embarrassing mistake.

Since that day, I've learned my lesson. Now I insist on obtaining clear pictures of the cats I'm sitting to avoid any further cases of mistaken identity.

***

My next tale is both strange and poignant. It all began when I had the pleasure of meeting a new client and conducting our initial meet and greet. Yet again, the cat was nowhere to be found during our rendezvous, but at least this time I had a photo of him (like I say, I'd learned my lesson).

My client was going away the following Monday morning and I diligently arrived at her house that evening to feed her cat. As per my instructions, I set out two bowls of biscuits and a generous offering of ten Dreamies. With the water bowl filled to the brim, I swung open the patio door, hoping to summon the enigmatic feline with a beckoning call. Alas, no response. Undeterred, I ventured into the garden in the hope that he was lurking in the shadows, unaware of my arrival. Frustratingly, my calls continued to go unheeded. After a fruitless twenty minutes, I reluctantly went home, hoping to meet the elusive cat the following evening. But when I returned to the house, the scene was unchanged. The two bowls of biscuits and the ten Dreamies, which I counted out again, sat untouched, as if frozen in time. Naturally, a wave of worry washed over me. It's always a cause for concern when a cat abstains from their usual eating routine. Could they be lost, injured, or stuck somewhere? Or, in less distressing circumstances, perhaps they had developed a taste for the gourmet delicacies at a neighbouring abode or were off exploring the world, to return home at their own convenience. Fuelled by a mixture of concern and determination, I swung open the patio doors once more, clutching a packet of Dreamies to try and entice the cat in. Performing a symphony of shake-shake-shaking, I called out the cat's name, searching every nook and cranny of the garden. I then looked around the shed, peered among the plants and bushes and inspected the bins. I scoured every possible hiding spot hoping to catch a glimpse, or find a clue as to the whereabouts, of our mysterious feline friend. But it was all to no avail. The cat was nowhere to be seen.

Time ticked on, and there was still no sign of him. I decided it was time to seek guidance from the client. With a hint of trepidation, I composed a message: "Hi, I just wanted to let you know that I was here yesterday and today, but I haven't seen your cat at all. His food hasn't been touched. Is this usual behaviour for him?

The client's response hit me like a thunderbolt.

Hi Amelia,

I sincerely hope you're doing alright. It pains me to convey this heart-breaking news, and I can scarcely believe I find myself writing these words. Regrettably, my beloved cat was involved in a tragic accident on Sunday night, having been struck by a car. The devastating impact of this loss is felt deeply by my family and me. I feel an immense burden of responsibility for unintentionally leading you into this situation. It was my oversight entirely, as I was only informed of his passing last night. This unfortunate turn of events has unquestionably cast a shadow over the beginning of my holiday. Thank you for understanding and for your care during this time.

My heart went out to the owners, who had lost their cherished companion. Alongside their grief, I also felt a personal pang of sorrow, as I never had the chance to meet this beloved feline and share in the joy of a simple cuddle. Rest in peace, little one.

***

Another time, I was entrusted with the care of two, lively young cats. They were regular outdoor explorers who always returned promptly for their dinner when called. However, one evening, they failed to make their usual appearance, which immediately set off alarm bells. It was concerning enough that one of them was missing, but the fact that both cats were absent raised my anxiety to

a whole new level. I embarked on a frantic search for the duo, and for two, long hours combed the area tirelessly, desperately hoping to catch sight of their familiar faces. As darkness descended, I reluctantly had to halt my one-woman search party. Determined to find them, I returned to their house early the next morning, only to be greeted by an empty space once again. I resumed my quest, calling out their names with both anticipation and trepidation. Just as I was about to lose hope, I heard a faint mew. I quickly retraced my steps and repeated their names. To my immense relief, the mewing grew louder. I had found them!

My joy, however, was short lived. The cats had sought refuge in a locked storage garage beyond my reach. I immediately contacted the client and explained the distressing situation, and then I called the police. Unfortunately, they were unable to unlock the garage for me. Their suggestion was to contact the RSPCA and attempt to locate the owner of the block of garages. With a renewed sense of hope, I reached out to the famous animal welfare charity, only to be informed they wouldn't be able to intervene until 48 hours had passed. Determined not to give up, I made further enquiries and managed to find the contact information for the company that rented out the garages. A female representative from the firm duly arrived and documented the garage number, but due to policy restrictions, she couldn't open the door herself. Instead, she assured me that she would leave a note for the person who rented the garage, urging them to come and release the cats as soon as possible. As it was August and the height of holiday season, I feared they would be away as well. All I could do was wait. Consumed with worry, I tried not to think about the hunger, thirst and fear the trapped cats must be experiencing. Then my client returned early from their holiday, and though I was profusely apologetic, they assured me I wasn't responsible and promised to join forces with me to free their little family.

Finally, after three days, the person with the keys to the garage turned up to open it, and two famished kitties darted out, unharmed. It was a moment of overwhelming relief and joy – a happy ending to a tale filled with tension and uncertainty.

***

Allow me to share another of my cat-sitting escapades with you.

I'm usually a jeans and t-shirt kind of girl, but for my birthday, someone gave me an all-in-one jumpsuit, hoping to add a touch of femininity to my wardrobe. On a scorching summer day, I decided to give it a whirl, as it offered much-needed relief from the heat. Little did I know that this innocent-looking garment would lead me into a hilarious predicament. Now, this outfit had one minor flaw – it lacked pockets. And being accustomed to keeping all my essentials in them, it was a bit disorientating not to have any. But I thought, *It's just for today, I can manage without pockets for a few hours.* So, armed with my car keys, phone and the client's house keys, I went to her home and placed all three items on their breakfast bar while I fed her adorable cat, refreshed its water, changed its litter tray and spent some quality playtime with it. Feeling a sense of accomplishment, I decided to step outside to put the contents of the litter tray in the outside bin. However, when I returned to the door, it had sneakily shut behind me and refused to budge. I jiggled the handle desperately, realising that I needed the very keys that seemed to be mocking me from the other side of the glass. At that moment, I made a solemn vow to never wear that jumpsuit again.

Panic set in. As I didn't have my phone, I couldn't even call Dave. I looked across the road and spotted one of my client's neighbours, who happened to be packing up her car. I decided to ask if I could borrow her phone, so I could contact my husband. Thankfully, the neighbour was incredibly kind-hearted and not only gave me her phone but a refreshing drink, which was much appreciated in the heat. After hearing my plight, Dave assured me he was on his way. While waiting for him, the friendly neighbour had an ingenious idea. She decided to inquire with the other neighbours on the off-chance one of them possessed a spare key. She promptly went off to investigate, triumphantly returning a few minutes later clutching a key in her hand.

Overwhelmed with gratitude, I thanked the neighbour profusely for her invaluable help. I regained access to the house and made a mental note to share this amusing tale with my client upon her return from holiday. And when the time came, she couldn't help but find the whole situation rather entertaining.

In the end, the unexpected adventure taught me the importance of having pockets and revealed the kindness and generosity of neighbours, who turned an otherwise awkward situation into a heart-warming memory.

***

My next tale unfolded during the transition from winter to spring. My clients jetted off to Spain, assuming the worst of the winter chill was behind them. Little did they – or I – know that it would be back with a bite.

As I entered my clients' house the morning after their departure to feed their cat, I was greeted by a shocking sight – the entire downstairs was submerged in an inch and a half of water. It turned out that a pipe had frozen overnight, only to thaw out and burst, resulting in a deluge of water. Without hesitation, I called Dave and summoned him to the scene. He was with our daughter at the time and brought her along. Together, we embarked on a mission to salvage the situation. Luckily, Dave managed to shut off the water supply while I searched for the cat. I found him perched on a chair in the living room, mewing helplessly. It was evident that he was hesitant to jump down and risk getting soaked.

"Hey, it's going to be okay," I reassured him, before gently picking him up, cradling him in my arms and carrying him upstairs to drier ground, where he would hopefully feel safe and secure. Once settled, I took him up his meal.

With the cat sorted, I promptly contacted the clients to relay the unfortunate turn of events. They were understandably concerned and asked if I could arrange for a plumber to come round, which I was more than happy to do. Meanwhile, Dave and our resourceful nine-year-old sprang into action, embarking on a marathon effort to extract the water from the house. For hours on end, my daughter wielded a mop, tirelessly pushing the water from the living room to the hallway. From there, I used a broom to manoeuvre the water from the hallway to the kitchen, where my husband scooped it up with a snow shovel and hurled it outside. As the water level receded and became less scoopable, we resorted to dustpans and brushes, painstakingly sweeping the remaining water into the dustpans before transferring it to buckets. We then turned up the heating to try and dry out the lingering dampness.

Overwhelmed by the extent of the potential damage, my clients made the difficult decision to cut their trip short and return home early. They were deeply grateful for the effort we had put in to safeguarding their cat and cleaning up their sodden home.

***

Finally, in my most recent cat-sitting escapade, I encountered a truly mischievous kitten. After caring for her over a period of days, I realised that her greeting style was to bolt to the door whenever I arrived at the house to feed her. When she didn't do this one day, I spent a frantic ten minutes calling her name, darting from room to room in search of her. It was when I heard a faint jingle emanating from my clients' Christmas tree that my attention was diverted. To my surprise, I spotted something moving in there. Lo and behold, the kitty had managed to climb halfway up the Christmas tree and was now observing me from her lofty perch. While she found this undoubtedly amusing, I must confess, I did not share the sentiment.

Throughout my years in the business, I've had the pleasure of crossing paths with some truly remarkable individuals and their feline counterparts. From elegant Burmese and charming Ragdolls to majestic British and Russian Blues, and even an adventurous Savannah. I've had the joy of caring for a diverse array of cats, including all the delightful regular moggies in between. Each and every one of them holds a special place in my heart, and I take immense pride in the service I provide year after year. But what truly warms my heart is witnessing their journey from mischievous kittens to stunning adults. It's a privilege to watch them grow and blossom into their full beauty. Building a bond with each cat is a cherished experience. Some instantly embrace me as their trusted companion, while others take a little longer to warm up. But in the end, we always find our way to a beautiful connection.

Over the following pages, you'll discover snapshots of some of the lovely cats I presently care for or have cared for in the past. Left page: Pippin, Troy, Bal, Pablo and Avita, Lucy and Linus and Coco. Right page: Bal, Talisker, Kato, Cookie, Felix, Dolly and Lenny.

20

DE POEZENBOOT

pronounced "POOH-sen boat"; *poezen* is Dutch for cats

For some time, a question had been lurking in the back of my mind. Which countries out there are truly cat crazy? Desperate for answers, I decided to discover these feline-loving lands first-hand and immerse myself in their culture. It was a journey I knew would leave an everlasting impression, which I would treasure forever and share with my fellow cat enthusiasts. My exploration began with a virtual trip to Japan and a unique island just for cats. The secluded paradise, called Aoshima, in southern Japan, is mostly home to felines, who share it with only a handful of humans. Can you imagine? A utopia where lots of felines roam free, basking in the island's beauty. It was my dream come true – somewhere where I could be surrounded by a multitude of furry friends. As much as the cat island tugged at my heartstrings, the reality of its distance and my limited travel experience made it feel like too giant a leap. Undeterred, I shifted my focus, hoping to find a cat-centric haven closer to home. And by a stroke of fortune, my online research led me to De Poezenboot – a one-of-a-kind canal boat in Amsterdam that is home to fifty felines. I had so many questions. Did these cats truly call the boat their home, or were they able to come and go as they pleased? Was there a caring soul onboard, steering the boat through the canals, while the cats sat elegantly by the side, donning their personalised lifejackets? Could these feline friends genuinely enjoy a life on the water? And who was the brilliant mind behind the idea to house cats on a boat? The story behind De Poezenboot fascinated me. Determined to witness this extraordinary floating sanctuary with my own eyes, I reached out to the person in charge, a remarkable woman named Judith, who invited me to visit the boat in person.

I was filled with excitement as I arrived in Amsterdam, ready to visit the world's only floating cat sanctuary. Judith greeted me warmly and led me onto the boat, which was much bigger than I had expected. As soon as I boarded, I could sense the feline energy in the air. Before me was a sprawling expanse adorned with cat posts, numerous fluffy beds, and ledges where the cats lounged in utter contentment. Most of the cats seemed friendly, and though a few exhibited a touch of wariness, this only added to their unique personalities. The boat was fitted with a cat flap, granting them access to a walkway that hugged the canal side. From there, they could bask in the sunshine, feel the gentle breeze against their fur and observe the passing ducks and the ebb and flow of city life. Although the exterior of the boat was safeguarded with wire, I could see that the space available provided plenty to keep the cats entertained. As tourist boats cruised by, the animals became the centre of attention. People would eagerly snap photos, their tour guides weaving tales about the remarkable floating cat sanctuary, which is often referred to as an ark, something which resonated with me at a profound level.

As I chatted with Judith, a Persian cat called Kasumi leapt onto my lap, yearning to be part of our exchange. It was in this intimate setting that I delved deeper into the boat's origins and the effort required to sustain its remarkable existence.

The origins of De Poezenboot date back to 1966, when a woman called Mrs Van Weelde discovered an abandoned cat with kittens near her home and compassionately took them in. Word spread, and soon she found herself caring for more and more stray felines. People recognised her as the local, devoted 'Cat Lady'. However, as the number of cats in her care grew, her house became too small to accommodate them all. So, in 1968, Mrs Van Weelde made a visionary decision and purchased a boat for her cats. Her mission was to welcome felines of all types and provide them with a safe haven. Judith was one of the first volunteers to work on the boat, and she played a pivotal role in its journey. When Mrs Van Weelde grew too frail to care for all the cats, Judith stepped in and took over, continuing her work when her predecessor sadly passed away in 2005, at the age of 90. Listening to Judith's account, I couldn't help but be moved by the kindness that resonated throughout the story. Mrs Van Weelde's unwavering determination to rescue cats, and her ingenious solution of caring for them on a boat, struck a deep chord. And Judith, as the torchbearer of Mrs Van Weelde's vision, deserved the upmost respect for carrying on the mission and keeping the dream alive. It was a reminder of the enduring power of love and compassion, and the indomitable spirit of those who dedicate their lives to our feline friends.

Judith went on to share the intricacies of running and maintaining the floating sanctuary – a true labour of love that demands unwavering dedication on a daily basis. She opened up about the unique challenges they face, especially with the cats who are born to strays and are therefore unfamiliar with human contact. Initially, these feline newcomers arrive trembling with fear but, through meticulous care and patience, Judith and her team are able to gradually coax them out of their shells. Once these precious souls feel secure, they are prepared for a new chapter in their lives – a loving forever home. My admiration grew as I witnessed first-hand the rehabilitation and rehoming efforts undertaken at De Poezenboot. The sheer amount of work poured into creating the best possible lives for every cat they rescue was awe-inspiring. It was a testament to the team's unwavering dedication and their genuine desire to make a difference to the lives of these cats.

The cats for whom an immediate forever home can't be found stay on the boat until the perfect match is located. Some cats face unique challenges, including wild tendencies, emotional issues, or insufficient litter training – all of which require specialised care and attention. But the motto of De Poezenboot remains steadfast: to help cats wherever they can, ensuring a brighter future for each and every one of them.

An astonishing statistic revealed the magnitude of De Poezenboot's impact. On average, approximately 250 cats are rehomed every year – thanks to the tireless dedication of the entire team.

Following my enlightening chat with Judith, I had the opportunity to meet some of the cats. In one corner, a cluster of kittens huddled together, still untrusting of the humans around them. Respectful of their fragile state, I greeted them with a gentle acknowledgement before moving on, allowing them the time and space they needed to adjust. Nearby, cages housed the newly arrived adult cats, while another set of cages accommodated the ones who had already found their forever homes and were awaiting collection. Among those, I met two grey sisters who had forged an unbreakable bond; it warmed my heart to witness their shared journey, knowing they would embark on their new chapter together, never to be parted.

After meeting all the cats, I couldn't help returning to Kasumi, whose sweet nature and undeniable charm had truly won me over. She revelled in cuddles and affection, and her fur was meticulously maintained and luxuriously fluffy. I couldn't resist taking a photograph of her but, to my amusement, the image I caught portrayed her with an air of grumpiness, which was a complete misrepresentation of her true character. Judith revealed that Kasumi had been rehomed multiple times in the past, but her occasional aversion to using the litter tray meant that she was sadly always returned. Surprisingly, while on the boat, her toilet habits were exemplary. I would have welcomed Kasumi into my home in a heartbeat but, at 11 years old, she had developed a sense of belonging at De Poezenboot that I didn't want to disrupt with a long journey to the UK. As I stroked her lovely fur, I promised her that should I be lucky enough to return to Amsterdam, she would claim the top spot on my list of feline friends to visit.

Although Kasumi was full of vitality, I asked Judith about the cats who weren't blessed with good health. Judith explained how they had formed a valuable network of veterinarians who lent their expertise, albeit not without cost. Nevertheless, they extended a generous discount to support the feline residents. In instances where a cluster of cats fell ill simultaneously, or a group of four or five required vaccinations, one of these compassionate vets would even make a houseboat call, ensuring the cats received the necessary care without having to leave their floating sanctuary.

While De Poezenboot has always been a place of interest for visitors, it has more recently witnessed an unprecedented surge in attention, largely attributed to the power of the internet and social media. Once limited to devoted cat enthusiasts who had stumbled upon the sanctuary in magazines, the reach has expanded exponentially. This extra attention brings with it both positives and negatives. A new breed of tourist has emerged – individuals who seek a fleeting encounter with a boat full of cats for the sake of a selfie, before swiftly moving on. This shallow engagement saddens Judith, for De Poezenboot is far more than a mere spectacle. The overwhelming influx of visitors has necessitated the implementation of a reservation system, ensuring that everybody has the opportunity to witness the remarkable work being done on behalf of Amsterdam's abandoned cats. It was disheartening to hear how some people disregard the true essence of De Poezenboot, and see it as nothing more than a tourist attraction to tick off their list.

During our conversation, Judith went about the task of feeding the cats. I watched as the feline residents emerged from their cosy beds and hidden nooks to congregate for their communal feast. It was heart-warming to witness these cats, all with different personalities and backgrounds, harmoniously enjoying their meals side by side. Amidst this sea of whiskers and purrs, one cat, Rif, stood out. With a quirky charm, he skilfully used his paw to scoop his food from his bowl and onto the floor, before savouring each morsel. As I watched all the cats, I didn't pick up on any discord or tension; a peaceful coexistence prevailed, as each animal knew not to stray from its individual feeding spot. And there in the delightful commotion, I caught sight of Kasumi, who was perched on a ledge next to a picture of herself and gracefully enjoying her food.

The heart and soul of De Poezenboot lies in the volunteers' unwavering devotion to finding the perfect homes for their feline residents. Judith and her team prioritise the wellbeing of the cats above all else. Their needs always take precedence – a principle I wholeheartedly believe should be upheld in all aspects of life. Before a cat is rehomed, they undergo a comprehensive process that includes neutering, vaccination and microchipping. I deeply admire this practice, as my own cats have gone through the same essential procedures. I believe the practice should be universally embraced, as it could help curb the staggering number of stray and feral cats. One aspect of Judith's work that struck me the most was her dedication to the cats' happiness even after they have been rehomed. If, for any reason, the new owner finds themselves unable to care for the cat, or if the match proves to be incompatible, Judith welcomes them back without hesitation. Her commitment serves as a safety net, ensuring that each feline resident will always have a loving home. This level of care and consideration sets De Poezenboot apart from many of the rehoming centres I've visited, showcasing Judith's genuine dedication to the best interests of the cats.

Despite a reputation for avoiding water, the cats of De Poezenboot have adapted remarkably well to their unique floating sanctuary. They confidently roam the boat, often perching on the edge of the deck to observe the world around them, while remaining protected by the safety of the chicken wire. It's a sight that perfectly captures the resilience and contentment these feline residents have found in their unconventional home.

As my interview with Judith concluded, I couldn't resist a visit to the reception area and giftshop, which was adorned with memorabilia. Eager to commemorate my unforgettable experience, I purchased two De Poezenboot T-shirts for me and Dave and a smaller one for my daughter. Additionally, I selected a collection of fridge magnets, stickers and, of course, a keyring featuring Kasumi. These keepsakes will forever remind me of the beautiful time I spent in Amsterdam.

De Poezenboot relies solely on donations from the public to sustain its operations. Without the generosity of donors, there would be no cat food, toys, heating and, eventually, no boat itself. Contributions made during visits and purchases from the giftshop contribute to the continuous upkeep of the sanctuary.

I consider myself extremely fortunate to have met Judith, who is a true embodiment of a 'Crazy Cat Lady'. In recognition of her and her team's dedication to assisting homeless cats, a percentage of the proceeds from this book will be donated to De Poezenboot.

Here is a collection of photos that capture the essence of my visit to the boat and serve as a visual testament to the volunteers' remarkable mission.

21
KAY AND HER CAT CAFÉ WHISKERS & CREAM

When I began writing this book, I knew I had to feature a cat café because the concept is one of sheer brilliance. Cats thrive on attention, and people adore their charming company. It's a win-win situation for all involved. I reached out to Kay, the owner of Whiskers & Cream, a cat café in Archway, North London, and she kindly agreed to let me interview her, visit her café, and meet her resident cats.

When I arrived, I noticed the café's sign first, appreciating the clever simplicity of the wordplay. Yet, it was the ampersand symbol that truly caught my eye. Skilfully crafted to resemble a cat's head, complete with ears and whiskers, it added a special touch and injected the café's name with genuine character. The unmistakable sign, accompanied by the sight of a beautiful cat perched in the window, could leave no doubt in the minds of passers-by about the establishment's purpose.

Entering the café, Kay warmly greeted me in the foyer. I noticed a second door separating the cats from the front door, and Kay explained that they kept this one closed to ensure their safety. She then led me to the main café area, and I immediately felt at home. The interior was lovely – a large window at the front allowed the cats to bask in the sunshine and observe the world outside. A scratching post stood tall, providing a gateway to an elevated ledge.

I watched as one of the cats, Oscar, a striking, cream-coloured Tonkinese, seized the opportunity to climb to the top, as the café's visitors paused what they were doing to take photos. I went over to stroke him, and he radiated a contented energy, as though he were a seasoned celebrity accustomed to such adoration.

One of Kay's waitresses led me to my seat, handed me a menu, and went over the guidelines for my visit. I learned that a total of 10 cats 'work' at the café – four pedigrees and six rescues.

I was then introduced to Amelia, a gorgeous brown tabby. As a fellow Amelia, I felt honoured to make her acquaintance. The waitress explained that she is a shy cat who had found solace in the company of the Maine Coons when she first arrived at the café. Grateful for their support, they had formed a close bond, and she continues to spend her time with them.

Next, the spotlight shone on Winnie, a lovely black, fluffy cat, whose coat seemed to turn an exquisite chocolate brown when caught in the sun's glare. She appeared quite cautious and shy, but I was assured that once warmed up to a new human, she wholeheartedly revels in the attention bestowed upon her.

The sibling duo, Arti and Winnie, were a playful pair. I watched with a smile as Arti repeatedly dashed under chairs, seemingly chasing invisible prey. The waitress explained how he adored both people and food and would wear a pitiful expression if he felt he hadn't been fed on time.

Ollie, the newest addition to the feline family, captivated me with his pristine white and tabby coat, which was complemented by green eyes. He was rescued by a compassionate café staff member after being abandoned in a cat box, next to a note from the owner explaining how they had been evicted from their home. After receiving essential medical care, Ollie had gratefully embraced the cat café as his new abode.

Vanilla, the oldest member of the family, is another tabby and white moggy. Sadly, he was mistreated by previous owners and can only tolerate being touched on his head, which I had the privilege to do, witnessing a glimmer of contentment in his eyes.

Among the Maine Coons, I was introduced to Jack, who is distinguished by his slightly greyer coat and a white patch on his back. His sibling, Jasper, sports a browner hue and coarser fur. Both cats gave off an aura of warmth and friendliness, and, with their immense size and fluffy coats, immediately won me over.

Trixie, a mischievous Devon Rex, is certainly unique in appearance. Her white body contrasts strikingly against her black face, ears and paws. While her full name is Beatrix, I saw how her nickname Trixie aptly captures her spirited nature. Despite her petite size, it was clear she takes pride in asserting her authority and reminding everyone who is the boss.

Finally, I met Molly-Rose, a Tortoiseshell with beautiful patterns in her fur, who loved being tickled under her chin.

The rules governing the cats are straightforward: no feeding them, no lifting them off the ground and, of course, no touching Vanilla anywhere other than his head. These guidelines ensure the wellbeing and comfort of the café companions.

Following my delightful encounter with the cats, Kay joined me for a cuppa and to share her extraordinary story with me.

After spending 22 years as a senior psychiatric nurse in the NHS, Kay had reached a point in her life where she felt the need for a change. She was unsure of her next path when she went on a birthday trip to the Lake District with her friends. As they chatted, the idea of opening a café and baking her own cakes surfaced. To Kay it was only a passing thought, but the following morning, her friends surprised her by taking her to a cat café. The

experience opened up the possibility of creating her own haven for cat enthusiasts. Her lifelong love for cats and her passion for baking merged into a singular vision. With careful consideration, Kay decided that this was the moment to embark on the exciting new journey she'd been longing for. However, the path ahead proved challenging from the outset. Securing the lease for the café turned out to be a lengthy process, and the builders that had been recommended to her consistently let her down, extending the café's expected completion time from six weeks to a gruelling six months. Frustrated by the delay, Kay had no choice but to hire a new team of builders and incur additional costs.

The next hurdle on the journey was finding the perfect cats to inhabit the café. The process was far from straightforward. Kay initially reached out to rescue centres, but their stringent guidelines meant a suitable match couldn't be made. Undeterred, Kay explored alternative avenues and scoured online platforms where cats were offered for free. Vanilla was the first feline to join Kay's team. His previous owners had relocated and couldn't take him along, leaving him traumatised. Through devoted care and attention, Kay managed to transform him into a sociable companion – an inspiring testament to the power of love and patience. Winnie and Arti followed. The pair were initially nameless and plagued by fleas, but Kay swiftly gained control of the situation to prevent the infestation from spreading. Then came Amelia, who Kay had spotted numerous times in a pet shop, confined to a cramped crate. She had been unable to find a home until Kay came along. Molly-Rose's journey was marked by fear and trauma, having come from a hoarder family. Kay provided her with a safe space, even bottle feeding her in the early days to nurture a sense of trust and security. These five remarkable rescues found solace and love in Kay's care.

Recognising that people are drawn to unique breeds, Kay explored the pedigree market. A friend recommended the Devon Rex, leading to the introduction of Trixie. The prestigious Maine Coons soon followed, bringing an air of grandeur and distinction to the café. Kay observed how the pedigrees positively influenced the rescues, as they learned valuable play behaviours from them, which they had no doubt missed picking up as kittens.

With the cats settled, the café officially opened at the start of 2019, but then fate dealt Kay a devastating blow. Just months after opening, burglars broke in. The safe was torn from the wall, the doors forced inward, and the front windows shattered. I empathised with the heartbreak Kay must have experienced and, of course, I was concerned how the cats had coped during such a traumatic event. Kay reassured me that each one had instinctively found a safe hiding spot away from the commotion. Despite the doors being left open, none of them had fled the premises.

Then, in 2020, Kay was forced to close due to the Covid-19 pandemic. They say bad things happen in threes, and I sincerely hoped that this marked the end of Kay's streak of misfortune. Despite everything, her resilience shone through, her positivity proof of her pride in what she has achieved and her unwavering belief that this is the journey she was destined to take.

I asked Kay if the cats have a quiet retreat to escape the hustle and bustle of the café when they want some solitude. She assured me that they have their own private rooms, where they can go whenever they please. Furthermore, within the café itself, she has strategically placed elevated areas from where the cats can observe their surroundings without being touched. However, Kay added that most of the time, the cats eagerly seek out the company of people and revel in the affection showered upon them.

If you're a cat lover, I wholeheartedly recommend a visit to a calming cat café. Whiskers & Cream offers ninety-minute sessions that can be easily booked through their user-friendly website. For those seeking a shorter visit, walk-ins are accepted, particularly during less busy times. However, it is essential to book in advance for children, as the number of young visitors is restricted.

My visit to Kay's remarkable café left me with so many memories. It was beautiful to witness the cats being their authentic selves, blissfully unaware of how fortunate they are.

To learn more about Whiskers & Cream, visit their website at www.whiskersandcream.com or their Facebook page at www.facebook.com/whiskersandcream

22

ROME CAT SANCTUARY

While in Amsterdam for my visit to De Poezenboot, I embarked on yet another feline-related adventure, which all began when I stumbled upon a hidden gem – a cat museum defying all conventional expectations. Ladies and gentlemen, I present to you KattenKabinet, a place where cats reign supreme and humans are mere visitors in their kingdom. As I crossed the threshold into this fantastic place, I could practically hear a chorus of meows welcoming me in. The interior boasted ceilings so tall that even the proudest kitty would still need to crane their neck to admire them. And it was as if every nook and cranny had been meticulously curated to showcase the most enchanting cat memorabilia imaginable. These included cat posters, spellbinding paintings, intricate figurines, mesmerising sculptures, and a cornucopia of cat-themed books. It's not an understatement to say that the KattenKabinet had it all. As I meandered through the halls, I couldn't help but marvel at the palpable sense of feline history that clung to every artefact. And the best part? Real-life cats freely roamed the premises, weaving through the exhibits and guests. The museum made me determined to plan my next cat-filled adventure abroad.

And this was how I found myself at a cat sanctuary right in the heart of Rome. When I discovered the Torre Argentina Cat

Sanctuary online, I felt as if fate had conspired to combine my love for history with my obsession for all things feline. With visions of cats gallivanting through ancient ruins, I promptly reached out to the sanctuary's caretakers to arrange a visit. To my delight, they eagerly agreed. I couldn't contain my excitement as I marked the date on my calendar, mentally preparing myself for a historic adventure that would surely leave me with countless tales to tell. As I packed my bags, I imagined the encounters that awaited me amidst the ancient walls. Would I stumble upon a mischievous cat donning a toga and playfully pawing at a Roman statue? Or witness a moggy seated on the very spot where Caesar met his demise, plotting their own feline takeover? The possibilities were as endless as a cat's curiosity, and I couldn't wait for my trip to begin.

As I arrived in Rome, an unexpected downpour greeted me. However, I refused to let the rain dampen my spirits – pun intended. Armed with my trusty companion, Google Maps, I embarked on a quest to navigate the city's maze of streets. With each step, I wondered how many horses and chariots had thundered along these very streets in centuries past. Rome's timeless charm enveloped me, and I felt as if I had been granted a front-row seat to witness history unfold. While ambling along, I caught my first glimpse of the colossal Colosseum. Its grandeur and magnificence stopped me in my tracks, compelling me to pause and bask in its awe-inspiring presence. This architectural marvel stands as a testament to the ingenuity of the past and is an enduring symbol of Rome's rich heritage.

My journey led me through a labyrinth of cobbled streets and bustling thoroughfares until, finally, I arrived at the ruins of the fabled cat sanctuary. The ruins, expansive and exposed to the elements, were covered with patches of greenery and shrubs that seemed to reclaim their ancient territory. As I searched for the entrance, a delightful surprise awaited me – a tabby cat perched at the top of a flight of steps. I felt as if he had been awaiting my arrival and had been sent to guide me on my quest. Crouching down, I extended a hand to stroke him, feeling that familiar connection forged between kindred spirits.

Glancing towards the ruins, I spotted a black cat perched upon a tree stump, while another took shelter among the lush greenery nearby. Further up, two cats casually observed the world from the top of a crumbling wall, their nonchalant demeanour demonstrating the tranquillity they felt in their vast, open garden. These contented kitties carried an air of fearlessness, as if they were the rightful custodians of this ancient sanctuary. Descending the steps, I encountered a group of six more cats at the entrance. I crouched down, hoping to offer them a gentle stroke, but they seemed indifferent to my presence; a reminder that cats possess a mysterious independence that cannot be easily tamed. I spotted a sign reminding visitors of the sanctuary's rules, which included a ban on photography and filming. I then made my way to the reception area, where a woman greeted me to share the story of the sanctuary's rich history and introduce me to more of its feline inhabitants. Inside, a dozen more cats observed me closely. I listened intently as my guide painted a vivid picture of their noble cause and the ongoing efforts to care for the cherished cats of Rome.

The sanctuary had an admirable mission at its core: the sterilisation of stray cats that roam the ancient streets. Through their ingenious programme, aptly named trap–neuter–return (TNR), they had embarked on a quest to curb the ever-growing population of feline wanderers. This programme was the catalyst that gave birth to the sanctuary, and the caregivers' tireless efforts had resulted in the sterilisation of over 70,000 cats since 1999, when it was founded. I learned how the sanctuary served as a safe haven for cats who, for various reasons, couldn't be returned to their original territory. Some suffered from ill health or disabilities, while others had simply found solace in the sanctuary's serene surroundings. These fortunate felines had been sterilised and given their essential vaccinations, providing them with a chance at a healthier, happier life.

My curiosity piqued, I was eager to explore further. From the reception area, I could see a designated nursery – a sanctuary within a sanctuary – where recovering cats were lovingly cared for, until they were ready to be released back into the wider ruins. At the time of my visit, the sanctuary was home to 83 feline residents, with 20 of them requiring specialised, long-term care. While adoption was a possibility for some, certain cats presented unique challenges due to health issues or their more feral natures, making it difficult to find them suitable forever homes.

Typically, young, healthy cats find loving families more readily, but occasionally, a heart-warming connection blossoms between an older cat and an older person seeking companionship. I discovered how the sanctuary relies solely on the generosity of donations to cover its running costs. Visitors often contribute or purchase the branded items available in the reception area. Another avenue of support is the Adoption at a Distance programme, an ingenious initiative pioneered by the sanctuary that encourages people to sponsor individual cats. The programme provides vital financial aid to cover the care of the kitties in need of additional support. Through these means, the sanctuary can increase their impact and ensure the wellbeing of all their feline residents.

Within the ruins, the free-roaming cats enjoy a sense of autonomy. Cat flaps have been installed in the main door allowing them to come and go as they please, even after the doors have been locked for the night. I marvelled at the cats' harmonious coexistence. Each one had staked a claim to their preferred spot, observing me with a mixture of curiosity and aloofness. Some ventured closer, seeking attention, while others maintained a watchful distance. The ebb and flow of their comings and goings mirrored the dynamic nature of the sanctuary, as new arrivals replaced those who had ventured outside to explore. A dedicated team of caregivers, each with their own unique role, diligently attends to the feline residents' needs. Medications are administered, visits to the vet are arranged, and the adoption process is expertly facilitated. Prospective adopters are thoroughly evaluated, their homes scrutinised to ensure the right fit for both cat and human. The work that goes on at the sanctuary seemed never ending, especially considering it is open every day of the year.

I followed my guide towards the nursery, eager to meet more of the feline residents. As she opened the caged doors, she explained that the cats were kept inside for various reasons – some have disabilities while others require lifelong medication or specialised diets, so the nursery is their safe space. I spotted a magnificent scratching post at the far end of the room, which I knew would keep the cats occupied. Taking a seat among this feline symphony, I was immediately greeted by a charismatic cat with patches of tabby fur on his white coat. He seemed to have some sinus issues that caused him to constantly make a snoring sound that tugged at my heartstrings. Fearlessly, he leapt onto my shoulders, claiming me as his own, and continuing his gentle serenade directly into my ears. Just then, a delicate, pure white cat climbed on my lap, purring with huge intensity. I felt like the chosen one, and she seemed to find solace in my presence. Fragile yet full of love, she captured my heart within moments. Regrettably, due to her advanced age, the prospect of bringing her home with me seemed unlikely, though I would have done so in a heartbeat, as her affection left an indelible mark.

The nursery was home to many other remarkable cats. I also encountered a tabby with paralysed hind legs manoeuvring skilfully with its front paws. It demonstrated its independence by using a litter tray with minimal effort. Another resident, a black and white cat, was a testament to resilience, having lost its ears but not its spirit. I also observed a totally blind tabby navigating its surroundings with outstanding grace.

The sanctuary had provided all these cats with an alternative to the harsh realities of the streets, where their survival would be uncertain. Witnessing their harmony gave me a sense of joy and gratitude, as I knew that without this haven, their lives would be drastically different. Reluctantly, I bid farewell to the nursery and returned to the reception area, expressing my heartfelt gratitude to my guide and her team for their selfless hard work and commitment. I made my contribution, purchasing a jumper and two T-shirts, while also offering a donation – a small token of my appreciation for the profound impact the sanctuary workers have on the feline community. I stroked the cats in the reception area one last time, cherishing these final moments of connection before it was time to leave. I can wholeheartedly recommend a visit to the sanctuary, but for those unable to make the journey, exploring its website and perhaps even sponsoring one of the cats would be a meaningful way to support the cause.

The sanctuary serves as a reminder that acts of compassion can truly make a world of difference. We need more places like this, where love and care can transform the lives of those who deserve it the most.

23
LIL SCRITCH & MOGGY MANOR

Going on holiday often leads to unexpected and delightful encounters, but there's something truly special about forming a bond with a furry friend while on your travels. They can add an extra touch of magic to your vacation, but what happens to them when your adventures come to an end? This question has always lingered in my mind, which is why the story I stumbled on in this chapter resonated so deeply with me. Allow me to share the touching account penned by a remarkable woman named Rhia on social media. Let's just say it's a real-life holiday romance...

"While on holiday in Cyprus, my partner Stephen and I were befriended by a stray kitten, who ended up moving into our hotel room. We were sad to leave him at the end of our holiday, but we had no intention of bringing him home. However, as we were waiting to catch the coach to the airport, we got talking to another couple who informed us that the kitten's home, i.e., the hotel, was being demolished. The more we thought about it, the worse we felt for him.

"Once we got back home to England, we spoke to someone in Cyprus, who confirmed our fears and volunteered to try and catch him, but after several days, they still hadn't been successful. So, a few days later, I got back on a plane to Cyprus.

"Just minutes after arriving at the hotel, and armed with nothing but a bag of Dreamies, some fresh chicken and a cat carrier, I had the kitten in my arms. He had remembered me!

"Once settled, I called Stephen, who was at home looking after our other cats, and told him the good news.

"The next morning, I took the kitten to the vet to have his flea and worm treatment and his rabies shot, and then I waved him off as he went to his foster home."

***

Rhia's story might have a happy ending, but it was far from over, for she had no intention of leaving the kitten in Cyprus. Here, she picks the story up six weeks later...

"On 12th November 2022, I made the journey from my home in Norfolk to Manchester, where I was to collect the kitten, whom we named Lil Scritch because of his small size and love of being scratched, from the World Freight Terminal at Manchester Airport. He is now settling into British life with his four feline big brothers, who love him just as much as he loves them."

***

Reading about the profound goodness that emanates from some people's hearts, coupled with the bold risks they undertake simply because it feels right, filled me with admiration. In a world where numerous individuals would have overlooked the plight of a stray kitten, this extraordinary couple stood out, going to extraordinary lengths to make him part of their family.

Rhia's story burrowed its way into the deepest recesses of my mind, refusing to relinquish its hold. I felt the urge to personally congratulate the couple. So, without hesitation, I reached for my phone, embarking on a digital quest to contact Lil Scritch's

176

saviours. Rhia and Stephen responded immediately and invited me to meet Lil Scritch and his furry pals at their house, which is aptly called Moggy Manor. A date was duly set for a week before Christmas.

The three-hour journey to Rhia and Stephen's Norfolk home unfolded smoothly and, soon enough, I found myself on their doorstep being warmly greeted. As I stepped inside, the first feline I encountered was Morgan, a ginger and white Tomcat. He was perched by the window wearing a knitted Christmas jumper. Rhia explained that the windowsill was his special place, a perch from which he observed the world, rain or shine. Morgan's journey had not been without challenges. He had allergies that caused him to relentlessly scratch himself. During the early days of the coronavirus lockdown, he suffered a bad reaction to a flea bite, and then reacted to the medicine he was given to treat it. Morgan wasn't a fan of the so-called 'cone of shame,' so Rhia set out to find a solution that would discourage him from scratching and worsening his condition. In one of the few pet shops open, she discovered two small T-shirts especially made for pets. Rhia didn't think for a moment that Morgan would consent to wearing a top, but she decided it was worth ago. She dressed him in the tiny garment and was surprised that he seemed to enjoy wearing it, as if he was aware of its beneficial purpose. And she was even able to find an alternative to the cone of shame – a neck cushion in the shape of a doughnut, which was perfectly designed to prevent him from further irritation. He looked so cute that Rhia couldn't resist sharing his fashionable journey online. Whenever she posted pictures of Morgan donning a T-shirt and his cushioned doughnut, she got loads of likes, and Morgan became somewhat of an online celebrity.

As Rhia told me this story, another member of the Moggy Manor clan leapt onto the sofa, seeking attention. Bimble is a sleek, five-year-old cat with jet black fur. Rhia told me his full name is Mr. JB Dimbleby, which they abbreviated to JB, which stands for jellybeans and perfectly encapsulates his lively personality. Bimble seemed ever-so friendly and relished every moment of fuss and affection.

Morris, Morgan's twin brother, then shot past, settling by the doorway to keep a watchful eye over me. Rhia told me how Morris is a true lap cat, often favouring her lap above all others. Despite being half as large and heavy as Morgan, Morris possessed a solid build, as he'd been spared the allergies that plagued his sibling. Stephen had found the two cats living in dire conditions in a caravan and suggested to the owner that he and Rhia could provide them with a better home.

Henry, another member of the family, was a ginger Tomcat with a paler hue to Morris and Morgan. When he moved in with them, he devoured his meals with unparalleled gusto, inspiring them to name him after the vacuum cleaner. Henry had been a regular visitor to the garden of their previous home, and one morning they discovered him curled up with Bimble at the end of their bed. Determined to find Henry's rightful owner, they put up posters throughout the neighbourhood, complete with their contact information. However, as the weeks passed without any response, and with no microchip that would help them trace the owners, Rhia and Stephen decided to welcome him into their home. Despite his sweet disposition, a small trace of his feral past still lingered, and he continued to consume every meal as if it were his last supper.

Finally, it was time to meet Lil Scritch, a tabby and white cat. What immediately caught my attention was his beautiful eyes, which were slightly crossed, adding an adorable touch to his already off-the-scale cuteness. Rhia told me how they suspected Lil Scritch had a touch of Siamese heritage, which is evident in his almond-shaped eyes and a distinctive Siamese vocalisation when he occasionally meows. Lil Scritch observed me from the opposite side of the coffee table, his trust not easily granted. Sensing an opportunity to connect, I asked Rhia for permission to offer him a treat, which she gladly granted. As he gently took one from my hand, I understood just how Rhia and Stephen had fallen head over heels for him. Eager to showcase his prowess, he seized the opportunity to demonstrate his climbing skills and made his way up the Christmas tree with an air of mischief. Rhia revealed that due to the colder climate, Lil Scritch had yet to venture outside. As he sat by the Christmas tree, his tail gracefully wrapped around his paws, Rhia started to share his remarkable story while Stephen made us some tea.

Rhia and Stephen took their unforgettable holiday in Cyprus in September 2022. Seeking tranquillity, they chose the idyllic harbour village of Latchi, north-west of the island. Little did they know their vacation would be forever intertwined with the arrival of a remarkable feline companion.

Three or four days into their stay, Rhia returned from a local shop to an unexpected sight – a thin and forlorn kitten sitting in their driveway. She approached the timid creature, but it maintained a cautious distance while observing her every move. Gradually though, over the course of a few days, a bond formed. Whenever they went for a meal out, Rhia and Stephen would save some leftovers, which they tucked away in their pockets, to feed the hungry stray. Soon the kitten, whom they had already affectionately named Lil Scritch, was enjoying regular breakfasts and dinners, alongside his grateful mother. While the hotel had some resident cats, it appeared that Lil Scratch and his mum had stumbled across it on their travels and decided it was a good spot to try and find food. Revealing her feral nature, Lil Scritch's mother remained elusive and evaded direct eye contact with Rhia and Stephen.

Then Lil Scritch found his way into Rhia and Stephen's hotel room and made himself at home on their bed. From then on, the three of them became inseparable. However, amidst their newfound joy, a cloud of worry cast its shadow over the couple. Back home, Morgan had gone missing. Rhia and Stephen awaited news for two agonising days. Lil Scritch, seemingly sensing her sadness, nestled beside Rhia on the bed, offering her comforting presence. He seemed to intuitively understand that something was amiss. Thankfully, after a terrible 48 hours, Morgan was found safe and sound in a neighbour's shed.

As their holiday drew to a close, Rhia and Stephen bid a heartfelt farewell to Lil Scritch. While waiting to board the coach to the airport, Rhia expressed her desire to return to the hotel the following year, only to be told that it was due to be demolished at the end of the month. Rhia and Stephen were horrified, as it meant Lil Scritch and his mother would effectively be left homeless.

Back in the UK, the couple pondered their options, as they didn't want to leave Lil Scritch behind. Then Stephen remembered he had distant relatives in Cyprus. Although he had never met them, he decided it was worth trying to reach out to them for assistance. To their relief, it emerged these relatives lived a mere four miles from the hotel and were willing to try and catch Lil Scritch and bring him to safety. But after making an initial appearance, the relatives revealed that Lil Scritch had not been seen for three consecutive days. Rhia couldn't bear the thought of him suffering. An internal battle waged within her over whether to return to

Cyprus in search of him. The rational side of her mind questioned the feasibility, expense and potential disappointment of such a venture. Uncertainty loomed, and guarantees were non-existent.

When Rhia told her dear friend about her quandary, she proposed organising a fundraiser to assist with the associated costs. Although Rhia was hesitant at first, she decided to put the word out and observe the response. To her delight, everyone agreed that it was an endeavour worth pursuing. The outpouring of support exceeded all her expectations, providing a substantial boost to making their dream to find Lil Scritch a reality.

Ultimately, Rhia's unwavering love for the kitten triumphed and she booked a flight back to Cyprus. On the morning of her departure, she received a glimmer of hope in the form of a message to tell her that Lil Scritch had been sighted.

After a five-hour flight, in which Rhia was filled with excitement and a tinge of nervousness, she landed in Cyprus, where Stephen's supportive relatives were waiting to meet her, despite the late hour, with a cat carrier. She checked into the same hotel, increasing her chances of being close to Lil Scritch. Although weary from her journey, she decided to have a quick look around for the kitten before retiring for the night. She took with her a bag of treats, which she shook in the hope of grabbing the moggy's attention. Then, in a brilliant display of serendipity, Lil Scritch materialised and bounded straight over; he had recognised her! Overwhelmed with joy and relief, Rhia whisked him away to the sanctuary of her hotel room, where she showered him with cuddles and more treats. She then phoned Stephen to share the incredible news.

The next morning, Rhia messaged Stephen's relatives to tell them the good news and ask for their assistance in relocating Lil Scritch until he was ready to be brought back to the UK. They took Lil Scritch to their trusted vet, who cared for their dogs, where he underwent a thorough examination and was neutered, given his first round of vaccinations and fitted with a microchip. As well as knowing a good vet, the relatives put Rhia in touch with a friend who owned a cattery, who kindly offered to accommodate Lil Scritch during the six-week interval between certain vaccinations, including the crucial rabies shot. With Lil Scritch's future safeguarded by a network of caring individuals, Rhia was able to return home, comforted by the knowledge that he was in safe hands. Now, all she had to do was wait.

Finally, Rhia received the news that Lil Scritch would be flying into Manchester Airport on November 13th. Determined to make the most of the trip, she decided to turn it into a weekend break. She booked a hotel in Manchester for the Saturday night and then discovered that The Supervet, Noel Fitzpatrick, was hosting a book signing in the city. Rhia had already bought his latest book and headed to the event to get it signed and snag a selfie.

Although Lil Scritch's flight landed at 6.30pm, Rhia had to wait around for three hours while he underwent a vet check. After sharing the rescue story online, Lil Scritch had gained quite a following, and Rhia later discovered that six hundred people alone had been tracking the kitten's flight to the UK. Rhia jokingly referred to them as the 'Scritch Fanclub', and she was both surprised and touched by the level of interest he had garnered. She imagined the airline staff wondering why so many people were tracking the flight, which was the sixth most-watched flight of that day.

When it was finally time to pick Lil Scritch up, Rhia was told that rather than collecting him from the airport itself, she'd need to head to the World Freight Terminal. Feeling lost, a kind woman, who Rhia had got talking to earlier, offered to drive her there. At 8.30pm, Rhia finally got to hold Lil Scritch in her arms.

After his arduous journey, she was keen to get him home. There was thick fog during the drive back to Moggy Manor, but Rhia found comfort in Scritch's occasional squeaks and, when it was safe to do so, she managed to stroke him through the crate bars. Weary but determined, Rhia pressed on and finally arrived home at 1.30am. She had achieved something that had felt impossible and looked forward to showering Scritch with love and providing him with the best life possible.

Typically, cats are nervous and apprehensive when they first move into a new home. However, as soon as Rhia opened Lil Scritch's carrier, he jumped out and onto Stephen's lap, seemingly expressing his gratitude for the rescue. He quickly settled in, spending the first couple of days in Rhia and Stephen's bedroom to allow him to adjust at his own pace. Stephen even took a few days off work to ensure Lil Scritch would never be left alone.

After the first week, Rhia and Stephen introduced Lil Scritch to Morgan, and the two cats happily sat together on the windowsill without a hint of conflict. Feeling encouraged, Rhia proceeded to introduce Lil Scritch to Morris, who adored playing with him and the laser light dot. The following day, it was Henry's turn, although he seemed more interested in food and sleep, nonchalantly walking past Lil Scritch to reach his bowl. Lastly, came Bimble's introduction. He hissed at first, so Rhia and Stephen kept Lil Scritch in the kitchen, allowing both cats to observe each other through the door. Bimble gradually accepted Lil Scritch, and now the pair share a special bond.

Lil Scritch's presence has brought out the kitten-like characteristics in the other four cats, rejuvenating their playfulness. Observing them together, it seemed as if Lil Scritch had always been part of the family. Rhia explained how she and Stephen had wanted to bring Lil Scritch's mother back as well, but considering her shyness and Lil Scritch's independent nature, they felt it would be unfair to introduce her to an all-male cat household. Instead, they sent money to the local charity that had helped bring Lil Scritch to the UK and had taken over the care of the hotel's resident cats following its demolition. The funds would support Scritch's mother, ensuring she had enough food for a year and covering any necessary veterinary expenses. In addition, Rhia and Stephen decided to sponsor another Cyprus kitten called Casper. It was a relief to know that it wasn't just Lil Scritch who'd been blessed with a happy ending. And I wasn't the only one who'd been touched by the full story. A week after Lil Scritch had settled into his new home, Rhia received a phone call from her local radio station, BBC Radio Norfolk, requesting a live interview, which she was more than happy to grant.

As I prepared to bid farewell to the inhabitants of Moggy Manor, I turned my attention to Morgan and his fame as a fashionable feline. I wondered where Rhia had got his Christmas jumper. Rhia told me how inspiration had struck when she saw an internet post featuring a cat donning a hoodie with the word 'Purrvana' on it – a clever nod to the iconic '90s rock band Nirvana. They were sold by an online shop called Hoodcat in the US, and Rhia acquired a whole collection for Morgan, including the 'Purrvana' hoodie, and ones bearing the names 'Fur Fighters', 'Slipcat', 'Mewtallica', 'Purrl Jam', and the festive Christmas jumper he was currently sporting. Encouraged by the initial response to Morgan's fashionable attire on social media, Rhia created a dedicated Facebook page for him, which she aptly named 'Mogman's Wardrobe'. He has since gained a global following comprising thousands of cat enthusiasts. Rhia then had the ingenious idea to put together a calendar showcasing all Morgan's fashion shoots. She only intended to give them to friends and family, but she ended up selling two hundred and fifty and donating all the proceeds to local cat charities. Due to popular demand, the calendar is now an annual tradition, and Rhia has also ventured into selling Christmas cards, hoodies, T-shirts, beanie hats, tea towels, bags and lanyards. To enjoy Morgan's sartorial adventures for yourself, you can visit Mogman's Wardrobe on Facebook or follow his Instagram account @mogmans_wardrobe.

I am deeply grateful to Rhia and Stephen for welcoming me into their home and allowing me to share Lil Scritch's life-changing story with you. I hope it resonates with you in the same profound way it did with me.

24
CAT FACTS

Loving cats as much as I do, I have learnt some very interesting facts about them along the way, which I thought I'd share with you here.

- Cats have a third eyelid called a haw, which is generally only visible when a kitty is unwell.

- A group of cats is called a clowder.

- A group of kittens is sometimes called a kindle.

- Cats have 230 bones compared to a human's 206.

- Cats have a scent organ in the roof of their mouths called the vomeronasal (or Jacobson's) organ, which allows them to taste scents in the air.

- Cats have whiskers on the back of their front legs.

- A cat's nose print is as unique as a human fingerprint.

- The cheetah is the only member of the cat family that can't retract its claws.

- Abraham Lincoln was the first US president to bring cats into the White House.

- In Ancient Egypt, there was a time when cats were considered sacred animals and bringers of good fortune, and harming or killing one was punishable by death. When a cat died, its body would be wrapped in the finest materials and then embalmed. The owners would even shave off their eyebrows as a sign of mourning. They would continue to grieve until their eyebrows had grown back.

- A Maine Coon holds the record for the longest cat. He measured 48.5 inches long (123 centimetres).

- The longest tail on a domestic cat belonged to a silver Maine Coon and measured 17.58 inches (44.66 centimetres).

- The oldest cat recorded was called Crème Puff, and they lived to an astonishing 38 years and 3 days.

- Female felines are super fecund, which means that each of the kittens in her litter can have a different father.

- Ailurophile means a person who loves cats.

- Ailurophobia means a fear of cats.

- The maximum running speed of a cat is around 30 miles per hour.

- Cats are crepuscular, which means they are more active at dawn and dusk.

- Hissing in cats is defensive not aggressive. It's an expression of fear, stress or discomfort and communicates 'stay away'. If cats are fighting, the cat that is hissing is the more vulnerable one.

- Cats groom other cats, and sometimes people, in a ritual called allogrooming.

- Studies suggest that domesticated cats first appeared around 3600 BC.

- There are fewer than 100 cat breeds, though the number depends on who you ask. The International Cat Association (TICA) recognises 71 cat breeds, while the Cat Fanciers' Association (CFA) recognises only 44.

- Cats have 32 muscles in their ears and can rotate them 180 degrees.

- Cats walk like camels and giraffes; they move both of their right feet first and then move both of their left feet. No other animals walk this way.

- If a cat loses its footing and falls from a tree, it has the innate ability to twist the right way up before it lands.

- Cats can't taste sweetness.

- Cats spend 70% of their lives sleeping.

- An orange tabby called Stubbs was the honorary mayor of Talkeetna, a small town in Alaska, for 20 years. Although he didn't hold any legislative power, he was loved by the locals and tourists alike.

- The Guinness World Record Holder for the richest cat in the world was a pampered pet called Blackie. When his owner, Ben Rea, died in May 1988, he bequeathed his 7-million-pound fortune to Blackie, who was the last surviving of the 15 cats he had shared his mansion with.

- It's believed that Isaac Newton invented the cat flap. When he was working on his experiments at Cambridge University, he was constantly interrupted by his cats scratching at the door. So, he asked a carpenter to saw two holes in the door, one for the mother cat and one for her kittens.

- Approximately 200 feral cats roam the grounds of Disneyland, where they help control the amusement park's rodent population. They're all neutered, and the park's staff provide them with medical care and extra food. They generally stay hidden out of sight during the day and only come out at night. There are exceptions, of course, and guests have been known to spot them out and about. As a general rule, Disney doesn't encourage its guests to get too close to them.

- Cats can drink seawater, as their kidneys are able to filter the salt out of them, which is something that human kidneys can't do.

- Cats can make as many as 100 different vocal sounds compared to dogs, which can only make around 10.

- Cats' claws curve downward, which means they can't climb down trees headfirst and instead must back down the trunk.

- Unlike humans, cats have a free-floating collarbone that allows them to squeeze through tight spaces.

THE END

And that brings us to the end of my story. I hope you've had as much fun reading it as I have writing it. Currently, I share my life with four amazing cats, but it can be bittersweet to think about the larger-than-life characters who have passed on and made my home a quieter place to reside. There's no chorus of meows to greet me when I open the fridge, I don't have six cats piled on top of me while I'm trying to watch TV, and there are no more feline fiestas when I come home from work. The silence is something I'll never quite get used to, but the abundance of love showered upon me all at once is something I'll always cherish.

The quieter characters remain, and they are all loved beyond measure. Each one expresses their love in their own unique way, and I've learned to appreciate and embrace their individuality. The journey of having multiple cats has been a whirlwind of joy and a valuable learning experience that I wouldn't trade for anything. I have discovered that just like people, every cat is different – their personalities, habits, and even who they choose to entrust their loyalty with. Some crave constant attention, while others prefer their independence. But one thing is certain: no matter what's happening in your life, cats will always love you.

Sure, they've cost Dave and me a small fortune over time, but that's what you do for family, isn't it? The happiness they've brought into my life is immeasurable, and these precious memories will be forever etched into my heart. I hope they will stay with you, too.

So, it's time to bid farewell. Goodbye from me, goodbye from Isis, goodbye from Shush, goodbye from Shakira, goodbye from Ginge, goodbye from Shrek, goodbye from Zeus, goodbye from Ooshee, goodbye from Squishy, goodbye from Sushi, goodbye from Koshka, goodbye from Winter, goodbye from Katinka and goodbye from Daisy.

Thank you for joining me on this journey.

ACKNOWLEDGEMENTS

First, thank you to my incredible husband. You have not only been a wonderful partner but also a devoted father figure to our beloved feline family. Your compassion and quick actions have saved them during times of need, and your unconditional love has nurtured them when they have required affection the most. Furthermore, I am immensely grateful for your willingness to embark on countless cat journeys with me, enabling me to share these stories with our amazing readers. Your support means the world to me.

A heartfelt thank you to our daughter. Your love for cats and your enthusiasm for sharing feline adventures with me has brought me great joy. I am truly grateful for the cherished memories we have created together, and for the special bond we share.

I would also like to express my heartfelt gratitude to Nigel Dowse. Nigel, your unwavering support and willingness to be part of this incredible book have made all the difference. Your invaluable input on my first book, along with your magical photo skills on this one, has truly elevated their essence. I cannot thank you enough for patiently enduring my constant bombardment of photo ideas. Your creative energy and collaborative spirit have sparked countless light-bulb moments, and your belief in my success has been a constant source of motivation. Without your involvement, these extraordinary photos wouldn't have come to life. Once again, thank you from the bottom of my heart.

Another special thank you goes to my editor, Danielle, whose dedication and skill have brought this book to life. Thank you for not only embracing every idea I had but also for turning them into reality with such finesse.

A special shoutout goes to Hammad for designing yet another stunning front cover. Your patience and creativity have been invaluable. I'm truly grateful for your steadfast support.

Finally, a huge thank you to everyone who has contributed to this book, be it through interviews, photographs, or both. Your willingness to share your time and insights has been instrumental in making this project what it is. Your input has added a depth and richness to my book that would have been impossible to achieve without you. Thank you so much!

ABOUT THE AUTHOR

Amelia Hendrey is a devoted cat lover who enjoys the peacefulness of country life with her husband, daughter and their four cherished cats. Her days are a delightful mix of running her own cat-sitting business and pouring her heart into her writing.

When she's not busy taking care of her furry friends, Amelia crafts stories that captivate and inspire. She is also the proud author of two memoirs, *What Nobody Knew* and *Let Go of What You Know*.

In May 2024, she was selected as pet sitter of the year 2024/2025 by Prestige Awards.

Amelia finds happiness in the simple pleasures of a purring cat on her lap and the satisfaction of a story well told.

OTHER BOOKS BY THE AUTHOR

Available from Amazon.co.uk
Scan the QR code below for author profile.

Printed in Great Britain
by Amazon

46014079R00109